THIS IS NUMBER ONE HUNDRED

AND SEVENTY IN THE

SECOND NUMBERED SERIES OF THE

MIEGUNYAH VOLUMES

MADE POSSIBLE BY THE

MIEGUNYAH FUND

ESTABLISHED BY BEQUESTS

UNDER THE WILLS OF

SIR RUSSELL AND LADY GRIMWADE.

'MIEGUNYAH' WAS THE HOME OF

MAB AND RUSSELL GRIMWADE

FROM 1911 TO 1955.

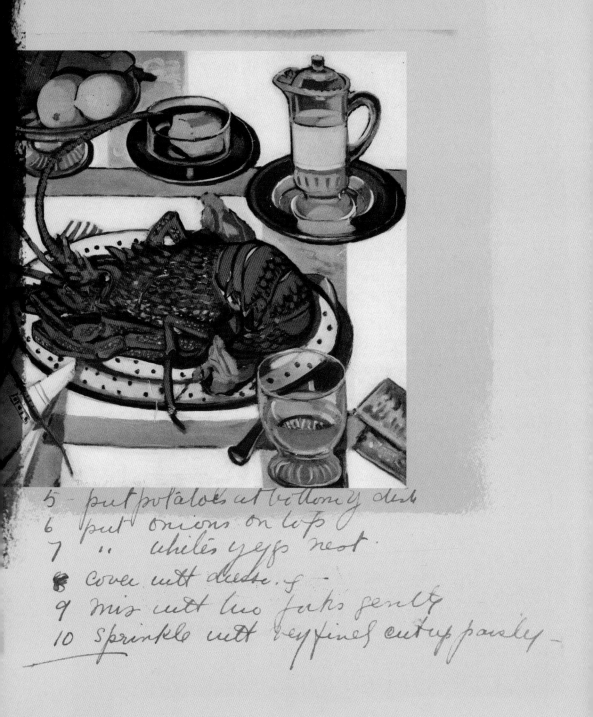

5 - put potatoes at bottom of dish
6   put onions on top
7   "   whites yeggs next.
8   cover with cheese. &
9   mix with two forks gently
10 sprinkle with very fine cut up parsley -

MARGARET PRESTON

Recipes for Food and Art

LESLEY HARDING

THE
MIEGUNYAH
PRESS

Japanese Scheme

C Ruby Red  1

D orange (reduced to brown)

E yellow (Primrose) 2

For Eliza

THE MIEGUNYAH PRESS
An imprint of Melbourne University
Publishing Limited
Level 1, 715 Swanston Street, 3053, Australia
mup-info@unimelb.edu.au
www.mup.com.au

First published 2016
Text © Lesley Harding, 2016
Design and typography © Melbourne
University Publishing Limited, 2016

Designed by Pfisterer + Freeman
Printed in China by 1010 Printing
International Pty Ltd

National Library of Australia Cataloguing-
in-Publication entry

Harding, Lesley, author.

Margaret Preston: recipes for food and art/
Lesley Harding.

9780522870121 (paperback)
9780522870138 (ebook)

Includes bibliographical references.

Preston, Margaret, 1875–1963.
Painting, Australian.
Art, Australian.
Cooking.

759.994

Page ii:
Lobster 1929 (detail), see page 106.

Above left:
Japanese scheme, Book 1—related to C major?
1920–24 (detail), see page 157.

Above right:
Tea-tree and Hakea petiolaris 1936
woodcut, hand-coloured
28.9 × 29.6 cm
National Gallery of Australia
Purchased from Gallery admission
charges 1986

CONTENTS

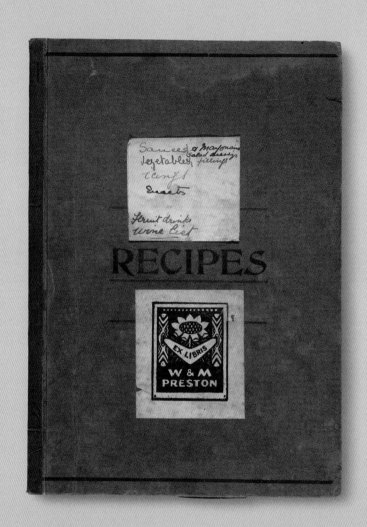

Sauces & Mayonnaise
Salad dressings
Vegetables, fillings
(cont.)
Sweets

Fruit drinks
Wine list

RECIPES

EX LIBRIS

W & M
PRESTON

AUTHOR'S NOTE

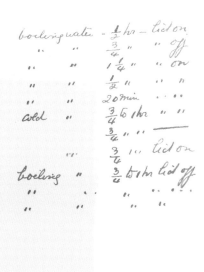

The idea for this book has been simmering since I saw Margaret Preston's charming volume of handwritten recipes tucked away in a solander box full of her prints at the National Gallery of Australia. That was well over a decade ago, and the viewing a chance aside during some research for another project. But there was something about this glimpse into the personal life of Preston, one of Australia's most celebrated and beloved artists, that registered the modest compilation as something worth further consideration at a later date.

In the intervening period my colleague Kendrah Morgan and I wrote a book inspired by a small, spiral-bound folder of recipes held in the ephemera collection at Heide Museum of Modern Art, where we work as curators. It belonged to the museum's founder, Sunday Reed, and the recipes formed the starting point for *Sunday's Kitchen: Food and Living at Heide*, a behind-the-scenes look at this well mythologised home and haven for artists. MUP's executive publisher Sally Heath was an editor at

Margaret Preston's recipe book
National Gallery of Australia
Gift of Mrs L Hawkins 1987

The Age at the time and made the brave undertaking not only to cook her way through the book's recipes, à la *Julie and Julia*, but to plant and harvest the required fresh ingredients as well. Her blog recounting the various trials and triumphs of the year-long project affirmed that food—its growing, cooking and sharing—can bring us closer to another time in history and to the table of someone we don't know.

Margaret Preston: Recipes for Food and Art draws on the same principles as *Sunday's Kitchen*, but the nature of Preston's papers and her extant correspondence—very businesslike, rather than revealing of her private world—required a different approach. Preston's well-known oeuvre is comprehensively covered by Roger Butler's major catalogue raisonné of prints and the definitive book on her paintings by Deborah Edwards and Rose Peel with Denise Mimmocchi. Their exemplary scholarship, together with the pioneering research of Mary Eagle and Daniel Thomas, revealed Preston's attuned domestic aesthetic and her democratic views about culture and craft. She wrote a host of articles on making art, from how to throw a pot, make a silkscreen print and weave a basket, to principles for decorating a house and arranging flowers. That Preston made her artwork at home, and frequently in the kitchen rather than in a studio, seemed to make these two styles of 'recipes' natural companions.

Along with the original recipe book (dating from c. 1915 through to the 1930s), there is a second tranche of Preston's recipes contained in a scrapbook at the National Gallery of Australia. These added to the possibilities for inclusion herein, while a clue in an article the artist wrote in 1930 helped identify the cookery book she purchased when newly married: Amie Monro's *The Practical Australian Cookery*. Monro's recipes cited in the pages that follow have been selected by instinct and supposition, but other than in one instance, it should be noted there is no firm evidence of Preston having cooked these particular dishes.

For ease of use the recipes have been standardised and metricated, and helpful notes from my testers and tasters have been added. Cooking times have also been adjusted to suit contemporary ovens. It will be clear to readers that these dishes are, on the whole, simple and unsophisticated fare, though they are typical of their time. That said, they call for ingredients readily found in most kitchens and I have added quite a few of the cakes to my repertoire. Like Sally with Sunday, I feel I know a little more about Margaret Preston as her home has come to mine.

A note on nomenclature: I have used the artist's maiden name, McPherson (which she also spelt 'Macpherson' for a time) until the point in the text where she marries and changes her name— aligning with the way she signed her artworks.

Lesley Harding,
May 2016

INTRODUCTION

Read all recipes through before starting to use.

No account of modernism in Australia is complete without due acknowledgement of Margaret Preston's contributions and originality. Recognised and admired for her vibrant and distinctive paintings and woodblock prints, she possessed an equally colourful, 'broad and bursting' personality, as her friend the artist and gallery director Hal Missingham once described.[1] Less well known is her legacy as a generous and insightful teacher, and her deep sense of civic duty. Refusing to adhere to conventional hierarchies Preston long advocated the making of a variety of forms of art and craft for both therapeutic benefits and edification. The appreciation and understanding of art, she maintained, had a liberating effect and served to draw the community together. She was also passionate about the need for a modern, relevant national culture that reflected local conditions and vernacular qualities. The building blocks of such a culture were not to be found in the pastoral tradition of art of the past, she believed, but in the homes of ordinary Australians.

The genesis of Preston's ambitions can be traced as far back as her art school training at the end of the nineteenth century, when she made an early decision to eschew the established idioms of narrative and landscape painting and focus instead on the more domestic genre of the still life. During her formative years she chose to paint subjects that were close to hand and often humble, such as fruit, vegetables, pots and tableware, finding the beauty in everyday things. In the 1910s and 1920s she exploited the decorative possibilities and colour harmonies in arrangements of flowers, and in the 1930s she captured the earthy tones and majestic beauty of Australia's native plants. Her cityscapes and scenes of urban life were those of her immediate experience, centred around Mosman and Sydney Harbour, as were her defiantly modern landscapes of the 1940s—remembered and composite images of places she was familiar with and connected to rather than grand vistas executed *en plein air*.

For much of her working life Preston abandoned the conventional studio in favour of painting and crafting at home, and often in the kitchen, where she could simultaneously attend to baking cakes for afternoon tea—her favoured time to entertain guests—or cooking the evening meal. While she held feminist views about the rights and welfare of women, and was committed and confident in the artistic causes she publically championed, these positions were underpinned by a quiet security in her private domain and an abiding practicality. She was a proud homemaker who enjoyed keeping an efficient and aesthetic house. She also enjoyed an equanimous and *simpatico* partnership. Margaret adored her husband, Bill, and in turn his devotion and financial largesse ensured Preston's art and wellbeing were nurtured and prioritised.

Travel was a mutual pleasure, and the couple journeyed extensively overseas as well as within Australia. Though undertaking many expeditions to exotic and unfamiliar shores, Preston was not a typical tourist. Rather, she was an investigator, a surveyor of culture and humanity, and once home again, a purveyor of wonders seen. Just as she shared her creative knowledge and techniques with students and the wider public, her adventures at home and abroad culminated in regular travelogues written for the popular press. Her appetite for seeing the art of other places was not driven by a desire to find ideas to imitate, but an opportunity to 'fill the well' and be able to return to her own work with fresh eyes and enthusiasm. Indeed, Preston's was a personal and singular journey in art from the outset, and while during the critical early period of her development she kept the close company of artists who were also intimates—painter Bessie Davidson, then potter Gladys Reynell—any mutual ambitions or overt influences were transitory. By the time Preston married and settled in Sydney in 1920 she had established her own idiosyncratic framework of preferences and parameters that would guide her art into the future.

In spite of her consistency of subject, Preston's practice never stood still; she was not only a constant student of art, but she was also prepared to take creative risks and investigate the aesthetic problems she set herself. Like Georgia O'Keeffe in the United States and Emily Carr in Canada, Preston forged a regional and intensely personal modernist language inspired by scenes, objects, nature, Indigenous art and later the landscape that were of private significance and readily available. As the academic Terry Smith has pointed out, like her North American counterparts she moved local possibility distinctively forward to create new challenges and solutions.[2]

Aspects of such a project were not without their controversy, however, for any of these artists. For Preston's part, as an early advocate for Aboriginal art, she made the misguided decision to promote the use of motifs found in bark paintings, carvings, shields and cultural markers as the basis for designs for textiles and decorator items for the modern home. She thought going back to the 'source'—to the images made by the country's First Peoples—would help define the way towards an identifiably Australian art. Preston's efforts in this regard have since been the subject of unfavourable review, and her appropriation of Aboriginal art has rightfully been criticised and censured for focusing on aesthetics and neglecting the spiritual and cultural significance of the originals. Her views changed and matured over time as her knowledge developed and her visits to remote Aboriginal missions, together with her involvement in the conservation of ancient rock carving sites, gave her first-hand understanding of the plight of Indigenous Australians and their culture. It has also been suggested that in championing Aboriginal and Asian art as a corrective to the European bias of art in Australia, she was an early advocate of multiculturalism.[3]

Preston's celebration of craft and the applied arts, traditionally seen as women's work, has received a more positive response, as has her parallel career teaching, lecturing and publishing on the methods and techniques of a host of artistic pursuits, from painting, printmaking, pottery and various crafts, to colour theory, flower arranging and interior design. Preston conducted her first art classes when a new graduate, and first began writing about the making and enjoyment of art in 1916. She lectured regularly to students and professional organisations, and reached a large audience through radio broadcasts from the early years of World War II. While she wrote instructive and critical texts for a range of forums, she enjoyed particular and long-term support from the publisher Sydney Ure Smith, and completed some fourteen articles for his *Art in Australia*, another nine for his next project, *Australia National Journal*, and thirteen for his long-standing monthly *The Home*, also providing illustrations and cover designs. This work helped keep Preston in the public eye and in no small way aided the popularity of her art, though her public speaking and publishing efforts were not simply a function of self-promotion. In these talks and exegeses Preston did much to demystify the making of art and crafts, and to encourage her listeners and readers to work creatively themselves.

Preston's experience as a teacher ensured that her instructions were clear and her tone authoritative. Fittingly, as Elizabeth Butel has pointed out, she seemed to shape her talks and texts in much the same way as she designed a picture: 'flattening the perspective and introducing patterns or rhythms that would benefit the overall structure, and not simply represent reality'.[4] Her 'how to' articles helped dispel the notion that art was an elite or leisured activity and reveal the faith Preston held in the liberating and civilising effect of art for the maker and in the home. These texts are recipes, if you like, not only for making baskets, pots and prints, but also for self and social improvement. 'Know your subject and paint your knowledge', she declared in 1941,[5] and this she did across her sixty-year career, intimately connecting her modernist vision with her domestic realm.

BEGINNINGS
CHAPTER 1

Now and again in the lore of art, stories are told in which an artist pinpoints a defining moment in their life when they felt a surge of creative power, and it appeared as if their future was pre-ordained. Margaret Preston had one such epiphany in her youth during a visit to the National Art Gallery of New South Wales, where the pictures on the walls, the smell of the polished floors and the whole atmosphere of the place awakened her senses and aspirations. Back at home, these innate feelings led to a somewhat audacious action:

> Once upon a time when I was twelve years of age I borrowed (?) my mother's best dinner plates and Brunswick blacked them all over. On to the blacking I painted flannel flowers. The result so impressed my mother that after the shock of the loss of the plates was over she determined to have me properly trained. Her justification was that as the flowers were the image of the natural ones I must have talent. From this on my imitativeness was well nurtured.[1]

This fortunate girl was born into a middle-class family in Port Adelaide, South Australia, on 29 April 1875, and christened Margaret Rose McPherson. She was the first of two daughters to David, a marine engineer, and his wife Prudence Cleverdon (née Lyle). The McPhersons moved to Sydney a decade later where 'Peg', as the family called her, attended the Fort Street School atop Observatory Hill, overlooking Sydney Harbour. After returning to the gallery to seek advice on finding a suitable art teacher, tuition was arranged for the budding painter at William Lister Lister's studio in Angel Place; McPherson was one of his

(opposite)

Margaret Rose McPherson in her Adelaide studio c. 1909

Photographer unknown
State Library of South Australia

(previous pages)

Nature morte (oignons) 1905 (detail), see page 7.

first pupils. An Australian-born artist, Lister Lister had not long returned from a long period in Britain, but soon became known for his naturalistic and at times romantic landscape paintings and seascapes. He insisted on working from life, so his protégé's first oil painting was an easy still-life assemblage with a striped tablecloth and coloured vase.[2]

In the early 1890s the McPhersons moved to Melbourne, where Margaret studied with Madame Berthe Mouchette at Oberwyl Ladies College and learnt china, fan and silkscreen painting, and a range of crafts; in all of these pursuits, flower studies were routine. She enrolled at the National Gallery of Victoria Art School, then Australia's most prestigious art college, in 1893.

The Gallery School was then under the formidable directorship of Bernard Hall, an Englishman who had trained as a painter in Munich. Though he had only assumed his post the year before, Hall cut a stern figure of authority, a bearing undoubtedly helped by the fact he seldom smiled.[3] McPherson's fellow student Norman Macgeorge remembered:

> At intervals of a few weeks or so the students would be invited to partake of afternoon tea in the master's studio and to view some of his latest paintings, which for the most part were realistic studies of the nude posed against backgrounds of brass trays [and] other appurtenances or lounging negligently still unclothed upon a settee ... We were all far too overawed to venture an opinion upon these works and usually sat in embarrassed silence as we balanced our tea cups precariously upon our knees and hoped we would not drop any crumbs.[4]

Hall believed the student of art needed a thorough and incremental grounding, achieving merit in each stage of their training before advancing to the next. Line, form, tone and then colour were perfected, with students drawing from the plaster cast before progressing to the life model, and finally graduating to painting in oil—it was a preparation to be endured rather than enjoyed. McPherson excelled, however, and was eventually elevated to work in the 'number one' studio among the most talented in her cohort, including Hugh Ramsay, Violet Teague and Max Meldrum. Frederick McCubbin, the drawing master, was nearly as apprehensive as the students in Hall's presence, like 'a naughty boy about to be reprimanded for something done amiss'.[5] McPherson, on the other hand, was daunted but not intimidated. 'I really started to learn', she recalled. 'Bernard Hall stamped drawing theory into my head, and ... McCubbin taught me fantasy.'[6]

Fate interrupted, however, when early in 1894 David McPherson was admitted to Parkside Asylum (now Glenside Hospital) suffering 'general paralysis of the insane'—a euphemism for tertiary syphilis. Prudence and younger daughter Ethelwynne returned with him to Adelaide, while Margaret saw out the first term at the Gallery School before joining the rest of her family. It was not until mid 1896, two years after her father's death, that she returned to Melbourne. In the intervening period she kept up her painting and exhibited professionally for the first time. The hiatus served her well, as following the resumption of her studies McPherson won a number of prizes at the school. She had already found her *métier*, preferring to work in the still-life

Nature morte (oignons) 1905

oil on canvas
44.4 × 63.5 cm
Art Gallery of South Australia
Elder Bequest Fund 1907

FRENCH JELLIES

30 g gelatine leaves

475 ml water

900 g sugar

pinch cream of tartar

flavouring essences
and colourings

Soak the gelatine in half the water for some hours.
Put remainder of water and the sugar into a saucepan,
bring to the boil, and add the cream of tartar and the
gelatine. Stir until the gelatine is dissolved and boil
for 20 minutes. Pour into wetted plates or dishes,
adding any flavourings and colourings. Allow to
stand overnight until thoroughly set. Next day, cut in
squares and roll in sugar.

*Adding rosewater or orange essence gives a
lovely result.*

From Margaret Preston's scrapbook

*When Guests
Come to Dinner,*

you should provide—

1.—Soup or Hors d'Œuvres.
2.— Fish or Entrée.
3.—Joint with two vegetables.
4.—Sweet Dish.
5.—Cheese and Biscuits.
6.—Coffee (Dessert optional).

Still life 1901

oil on canvas
45.1 × 60.1 cm
Art Gallery of South Australia
M J M Carter Collection 2004

room over painting Hall's 'hideous' models. 'It would seem that a liking for the colour and form of inanimate objects was born in her', she later wrote of her younger self.[7]

Although there was nothing new about Hall's approach to art education, he did possess a degree of enlightenment concerning the extension of art into daily life. He thought the development of a domestic aesthetic—the application of good taste and artistic judgement in the home—was a necessary skill in the wider community, and believed the fine and applied arts should be more closely aligned. This saw him introduce subjects in the latter into the curriculum of the National Gallery School in 1896. While he was a difficult principal and not a particularly inspiring artist, Hall should yet be acknowledged for his vision on this count, and for imparting to his students the necessity of craftsmanship—an ideal the gifted Miss Rose McPherson, as she was known by her fellow students, carried with her for the duration of her long career.

Upon graduating from the Gallery School in 1897 McPherson left Melbourne for Adelaide once again, and although already quite proficient as a painter, she enrolled as a student of HP Gill at the South Australian School of Design, Painting and Technical Arts. Gill had trained in England and brought aspects of the Arts and Crafts model with him to Adelaide. As in Melbourne, tuition in the applied arts was offered, including classes in pottery, china painting, decorative needlework and fretwork. McPherson also joined the South Australian Society of Arts, providing her with an opportunity for exhibiting, though she had by now determined she would earn her living through teaching and by

Still life 1901

oil on canvas
40.6 × 51 cm
The Royal Art Society
of New South Wales

Spilt milk c. 1903

oil on canvas board
32 × 39.5 cm
Private collection

MISS BROOME'S SALAD DRESSING

1 pinch salt

1 pinch dry mustard

1 pinch cayenne pepper

1 egg

285 ml oil

juice of ½ lemon

Put salt, mustard and cayenne pepper in a basin and break the whole egg into it; beat up well. Add the oil drop by drop (about six drops), beating well into the mixture. Add more drops of oil, beating well until the oil is used. The mixture will be the consistency of heavy cream.

If more than a few drops of oil are put in at a time, the dressing will not turn. Flavour with the lemon juice.

Margaret Preston's addendum to this recipe: must beat this dressing well with a ladle or double eggbeaters.

From Margaret Preston's recipe book

if more than a few drops of oil are put in at a time — the dressing will not turn.

Still life: lobsters 1901

oil on canvas
76.2 × 110.2 cm
Private collection

accepting portrait commissions; not her preferred genre but likely to attract firm sales. She rented well-located rooms in King William Street in the city in 1899, where she conducted lessons in watercolour and oils, finding time for her own work around an increasingly busy timetable. Her presiding theme was still life but even more specifically—and significantly—in those formative years, she painted objects that were readily available and straight out of the pantry. Potatoes, onions, pots, plates, vases and jugs, an arrangement of apples and celery, and a breakfast table with a jug of spilt milk were among her first independent subjects.

The majority of McPherson's early paintings bear the imprint of the Gallery School's tonal realism, displaying great poise and restraint. Her most elaborate oil from these years is the 1901 *Still life: lobsters*, an homage to seventeenth-century Dutch painting. It is a cornucopia of seafood and grapes embellished with drapery and dining accoutrements, carefully toned and coloured, and garnished with an exquisitely handled peeling lemon. This last, a motif borrowed from the Dutch, seems to project straight out of the picture and into the real world. But on the whole McPherson preferred an everyday reality in the mode of the French painter Jean-Baptiste Chardin, and more humble subjects, such as onions and eggs. Her renderings of the latter were so realistic that they were 'almost short of hatching'.[8] She had surely achieved her stated aim, 'to paint them with such fidelity to nature that they could almost be used in the kitchen'.[9]

It followed that McPherson's students would develop a similar aptitude for the domestic still life. At the third annual exhibition

of her little school, in September 1902, it was reported that all 180 works were painted directly from the subject; no copies allowed. Moreover, the flower studies were rated among the strongest exhibits and combined 'artistic taste with originality'.[10] At this time the still life was largely out of favour in mainstream art circles, and generally considered a feminine pursuit and a lesser art. The prevailing public and critical preference was for landscape painting and figurative or narrative pictures; if the images construed the conquering of the bush and a pastoral ambience, all the better. Fashions and trends would rarely sway McPherson, however, and this perceived opposition to her favoured subject seems only to have strengthened her resolve to

paint 'just everything she liked'.[11] Such thinking anticipated her later promotion of gender equality in the arts and the equality of art forms, in particular the integration of crafts traditionally undertaken by women into mainstream culture.

Margaret McPherson's Adelaide studio 1901

Photographer unknown
Private collection

While not highly regarded in Australia, the genre of still life had been undergoing a phase of reinvention abroad in the preceding decades, notably by the impressionists and post-impressionists. Soon after, it was the vehicle for great change in twentieth-century painting via Picasso and Braque's 'analytical' Cubism. In this mode the *nature morte* was dismantled and the fractured forms of its component objects shown from multiple viewpoints at once. It was a revolutionary and generative development,

POTATO CROQUETTES

potatoes, as many as
required for the meal

1 egg

½ cup milk

fresh breadcrumbs,
fried until golden

oil or butter to fry

salt and pepper

Boil the potatoes, or use those left over from a
previous meal. Break them into a flour or pulp, then
bind with some of the egg beaten up with the milk.

Make into balls about the size of a tangerine, then
brush with the remainder of the beaten egg. Roll in
the golden breadcrumbs and fry until brown.

Any of the usual seasonings may be used with
advantage.

From Margaret Preston's recipe book

*Peel potatoes very thin because certain
Calories are just underneath the skin
— These are mineral salts —*

offering alternative ways of picturing the world and opening up new possibilities for art. While for McPherson such revelations lay some years into the future, she intuitively understood the still life would provide sufficient variation and areas of discovery to occupy a lifetime.

By the time her mother died in 1903 McPherson had several years of teaching experience, but she was not yet finished with her own study of art. There was no longer a compelling reason to remain in Adelaide, and with the benefit of a small inheritance she commenced preparations to leave for Europe the following year. Bessie Davidson, a student and now intimate companion—and likely lover—decided to accompany her. Like McPherson, Davidson was of Scottish descent and possessed a stimulating intellect; she had also just lost her mother. The duo departed for Munich in July 1904.

Although travelling Australian artists usually had Paris in their sights, McPherson had warmed to Munich after favourable reports from Bernard Hall, and Davidson's father (who was providing the pair with a living allowance) thought it a more suitable and less bohemian destination for the young artists. Once there they enrolled at the Künstlerinnen Verein, a government art school for women. McPherson only attended a few classes before moving to what she referred to as 'the illustration schools', which likely means an atelier or institute for applied arts. She was nonplussed by German art, which she found alternatively staid or eccentric, and repelled by the country's reactionary social mores: 'the German attitude towards women is not progressive. Everything is for the men', she complained.[12]

They left the austere and disciplined atmosphere of Munich for the more liberal and progressive art scene of Paris later that year, forfeiting their stipend in the process.

After arriving in Paris the couple installed themselves in a small apartment in the Latin Quarter and made the acquaintance of long-term Australian expatriate artist Rupert Bunny, whose work they found impressive and whose practical advice had them studying at the Académie de la Grande Chaumière. Newly founded in 1902, this was a 'free' academy for amateur and professional artists, cheaper than Colarossi's—a popular choice among Australasians—and less strict than the École des Beaux Arts. Now with no outside pecuniary assistance McPherson and Davidson reported to an Adelaide newspaper that they made ends meet by taking on art students and selling paintings, including the whole of one summer's output to a Canadian dealer.[13] Both women enjoyed the honour of having work accepted by the Paris Salon in 1905, and the following year their paintings were hung 'on the line' (at eye level) alongside the most esteemed pictures in the exhibition. By the time of their return to Australia in 1906 they had visited England, Ireland and Scotland, Holland, Belgium, Spain and Morocco from their Paris base, collecting postcards in lieu of a diary. While McPherson did not stray from academicism in her art as a result of her travels, she did bring home some skills in poster design and 'new and curious methods of black and white drawing for reproduction'.[14] She also had her first introduction to the work of the Fauves, van Gogh and Puvis de Chavannes—an artist of great importance to Bunny for his decorative aesthetic, and a consummate painter of murals. These were all to be significant models for McPherson in the decades hence.

The tea urn (still life) c. 1909

oil on canvas
61 × 50.5 cm
Art Gallery of South Australia
Elder Bequest Fund 1909

Back in Adelaide, McPherson lived with the Davidson family—
she was invited for a weekend, and stayed two years—her forth-
right character and wilfulness surely altering the balance of
the genteel household. She also resumed teaching. McPherson
and Davidson took a studio in Currie Street in the city, offering classes in drawing and painting, and in December 1908
McPherson was appointed art mistress for the Methodist Ladies
College in Wayville, where the entire school art program was
under her charge.[15] Later she taught at the Presbyterian Girls
College at St Peters. This left little time for her own work, or for
extending her skills and style after her experience in Europe.
However, incremental changes began to arise: a wider and
richer range of colours, a lighter palette, and the first signs of
an interest in decorative visual effects. Gone are the rustic eggs
and onions, and in their place appear the plush trappings and
appointments of the Davidsons' upper-middle-class home: fish
bowls and tea sets, silver serving ware, and fine china. Her tri-
umphant painting *The tea urn (still life)* (c. 1909) encapsulates
the shift: colour is judicious but confident, balanced and lumi-
nous where required; the paint is handled with a slightly looser
touch and light impasto; and a bold organising scaffold of two
background panes in black and buff is utilised to good effect.
The urn itself is exploited for its surface qualities and aesthetic
appeal, the surrounding room abstractly reflected in its orb and
providing the focus of the arrangement—an intelligent use of
the still life as an aperture into the lived experience of the everyday world.

The meeting of subject and artist, artifice and real life was to
become a hallmark of McPherson's art, and as such it is possible

to develop an image of the artist herself through her paintings. She reinforced this as the key to crafting successful pictures in the classroom, as one student explained:

> We were instructed to set up our own subjects which quite often did not meet with Miss MacPherson's approval. I remember once I had arranged a study of a coloured bottle, some eggs and pomegranates all sitting up very sedately, but Miss MacPherson lost no time in cracking open the eggs, breaking open the fruit and scattering a few seeds around and then said 'carry on'.[16]

In 1910 Bessie Davidson returned to Paris alone, at which point McPherson found a new studio at 25 King William Street—and another intimate companion to share it with in Gladys Reynell, also a former pupil. She was one of five children born to wine-maker Walter Reynell and his wife Mary, part of a pioneering South Australian family credited with planting the state's first vineyard. Some seventy years later they were still running a commercially successful winery, Reynella, not far south of Adelaide.

Like Davidson, McPherson had set her sights on returning to Europe and had been 'penny-piling to be able to make a dash back'.[17] In early 1912 she departed once more, this time with Reynell as her consort. After a brief stay in London the couple moved on to Paris, where they were to spend the rest of the year. Contact was re-established with Rupert Bunny and they stayed with Bessie Davidson in her apartment at 64 Rue Madame, close to the Luxembourg Gardens. The period that followed was one of intense looking, reading and thinking as McPherson began her conversion towards a more modern outlook. She wrote to the

LEMON BUTTER

170 g butter
450 g sugar
6 eggs
5 lemons

Melt the butter and sugar in a saucepan. Add the well-beaten eggs, and juice and grated rind of the lemons. Stir until it all thickens, then put into sterilised jars.

If well covered this will keep for a very long time.

From Margaret Preston's recipe book

PASSIONFRUIT BUTTER

6 passionfruit
2 eggs
2 dessertspoons butter
1 cup caster sugar

Beat all the ingredients together well, put in a double boiler or jug in a saucepan half full of water and cook until the mixture is as thick as honey (around 30 minutes). Store in airtight jars. Good on bread or as a filling for tarts or sponge cakes.

From Margaret Preston's scrapbook

The fish bowl 1910

oil on canvas on cardboard
48 × 39.4 cm
National Gallery of Victoria
Purchased with the assistance
of the National Gallery
Society of Victoria 1977

artist Norman Carter in August 1913 that she was turning her eye to the 'decorative' possibilities of art inspired by Japanese prints and by the post-impressionists, 'the only thing worth aiming for in this our century—it is really the keynote of everything'.[18] McPherson was not referring to surface ornament or prettiness, but rather to an overhaul of pictorial design so that the whole composition is considered in terms of its constituent formal elements.

Colour presented a temporary impasse, as McPherson puzzled over how to move beyond tonalism and still achieve comparable expressive values, and then how to unite colour and form. If an emphasis on colour was not to spiral into abstraction, she realised, the artist needed to pay close attention to the rhythms of the picture and strive for balance. The new concepts registered immediately on her painting. Safe in her preferred subject matter, she painted *Holiday: still life* (1913) and *Still life: sunshine indoors* (1914) using pattern, a tilted picture plane, a higher key of colour, and a good amount of white in her mixing to achieve a bright and harmonious order.[19] Relating nature to geometry and purifying form were the next steps, and as a result analysis, rhythm and design replaced the earlier focus on imitation and naturalism. By 1915 McPherson was synthesising sumptuous colour harmonies, shallow space and an intellectual order in her compositions, while maintaining her objective faithfulness to the subject.

While in France she saw with fresh eyes the work of Puvis de Chavannes, Cézanne and Matisse. Gauguin also made a deep impression. On encountering one of his Tahitian paintings, *We*

Holiday still life 1913

oil on canvas
54.3 × 65 cm
Private collection

CIDER CUP

1 l cider
500 ml soda water
wine glass of sherry
half wine glass of brandy
juice of ½ lemon
lemon rind
250 ml pineapple juice
sugar to taste
nutmeg to taste

Put cider, soda water, sherry and brandy into a bowl; add the lemon juice and a small piece of the rind, then the pineapple juice, sugar and nutmeg to taste. Strain and ice well.

A refreshing summer drink with a little kick.

From Margaret Preston's recipe book

MINT CUP

Wash 3 sprigs of mint and put them into a jug. Add 2 tablespoons of sugar, 1 drop of peppermint essence, 1 drop of clove essence and a cup of crushed ice. Top up with soda water.

From Margaret Preston's recipe book

*Still life: sunshine
indoors* 1914

oil on canvas
52 × 64 cm
Private collection

greet thee, Mary (1901), she was captivated by its uncommon beauty: 'every colour, every line helped to balance each other, it was only small but so sure'.[20] It was around this time McPherson was advised (by Bunny or his friend George Oberteuffer, an American artist) to study Japanese prints, sculptures, paintings and ceramics at the Musée Guimet, 'to let her learn slowly that there is more than one vision in art'.[21] The experience affected her on two levels: the technical and formal qualities of the art she viewed would prove immensely influential on her work, while the process of absorbing another cultural tradition triggered a philosophical shift. She discovered, as she later wrote, 'that a picture could have more than eye realism. That there was such a thing as aesthetic feeling. That a picture that is meant to fill a certain space should decorate that space … That each century should have something of the characteristics of itself in its art'.[22] In time McPherson would readily translate this last idea to the machine-aesthetic of the modern era.

McPherson and Reynell spent four months over the summer of 1913 on the Île de Noirmoutier, off the coast of Brittany, before leaving for London, keen to 'explore other fields'.[23] A vibrant cultural scene awaited them, with British art, like that of France, in the midst of major change and renewal. McPherson, now aged thirty-eight, could not have been more ready for the challenge.

CRAFTS
THAT AID
CHAPTER 2

After disembarking in London in October 1913, McPherson and Reynell settled themselves in a studio at 5 Trebovir Road, Earls Court. By December McPherson was delighted to have her work accepted for exhibition at the New English Art Club, the first of a number of such opportunities to present her work in London—the Royal Academy and the Society of Women Artists were others. Established in the 1880s, the New English Art Club had become a well-respected exhibiting society, though just as McPherson was making her debut there, its status was under threat. Breakaway members formed the London Group and the Camden Town Group—both artist-led associations intended to counter institutions such as the Royal Academy—while a chain of significant events were transforming the prevailing cultural climate and 'revitalising' English art. The development of British modernism during this period greatly affected the advancement of modern art in Australia. In the right place at the right time, McPherson was among the first converted.

In the years immediately prior to McPherson and Reynell's arrival in London, the painter and art critic Roger Fry had orga- nised two landmark exhibitions of so-called 'post-impressionist' art—the term 'modernist' had not yet entered the lexicon— at Grafton Galleries. The first, held in 1910, showcased the work of Manet, Cézanne, Matisse and the Fauves, van Gogh, Gauguin, and the 'outsider' artist Rousseau; the second, held in 1912, included the work of the cubists alongside avant-garde Russian and English art. The Bloomsbury Group's Duncan Grant, Leonard and Virginia Woolf, Clive and Vanessa Bell, and patron Lady Ottoline Morrell were all closely involved. These groundbreaking displays were followed by the 1914 publication

(opposite)
Margaret McPherson and Gladys Reynell with Little Jim c. 1915

Photographer unknown
Margaret Preston papers
Art Gallery of
New South Wales

(previous pages)
Still life c. 1915 (detail), see page 37.

of a persuasive new book, simply and resolutely titled *Art*, by Fry's colleague, the art critic Clive Bell. In this Bell elaborated his theory of 'significant form', by which he meant the formal value of line and colour in a work of art that provokes aesthetic emotion. Significant form was art's essential quality, he maintained, and a connecting thread for the best creative endeavour across the ages. 'No-one ever doubted', he wrote, 'that a Sung pot was as much an expression of emotion as any picture that was painted'.[1] The book was to bring great influence to bear on the art of English-speaking nations for years into the future, especially as its advocacy of form over content provided a ready-made defence for abstraction, the next frontier in art.

Though McPherson missed seeing Fry's post-impressionist exhibitions for herself, she cannot have failed to hear about them. They had incited great discussion and debate in the press; indeed the aftershocks had reverberated as far away as Australia, where one news report bore the unfortunate subheading 'Art Gone Mad'.[2] On a more personal note, the collectors Sarah and Michael Stein, neighbours of Bessie Davidson in Rue Madame where McPherson and Reynell had stayed, assisted Fry with the 1910 show by securing for inclusion a major work by Matisse.[3] The combined impact of the exhibitions completely disrupted prevailing taste and the effects were immediate. Narrative and genre painting were made redundant, and colour, design and 'primitive' form were the order of the day. Fry's introduction to the second exhibition captured the spirit of the movement:

> These artists … arouse the conviction of a new and definite reality. They do not seek to imitate form, but to

EGG TOMATOES

large tomatoes—
1 for each person

breadcrumbs

eggs—1 for each tomato

salt and pepper to taste

Cut off a slice from the top of each tomato. Scoop out the pulp carefully, sprinkle the inside with salt, and drain out the surplus moisture by turning the fruit upside-down. Put a teaspoon of seasoned breadcrumbs in the bottom of each of the tomatoes, break a fresh egg into each, sprinkle with salt and pepper, and place on a tray. Bake in a hot oven until the egg is set.

From Margaret Preston's recipe book

BUY LIGHT HANDY
SAUCEPANS WHICH
WILL BOIL QUICKLY.
If you select those made
of aluminium, never
wash them with soda.

CHICKEN PIE

2 chicken breasts

flour

salt and pepper

2 hard-boiled eggs

125 g mild ham

1 dessertspoon
chopped parsley

1 dozen mushrooms

1 cup stock,
approximately

cornflour

225 g puff pastry

1 egg, extra

Cut chicken into neat pieces and dip in flour, pepper and salt. Slice eggs thinly and cut ham into neat slices. Arrange all in a pie dish in alternate layers of chicken, ham and eggs, sprinkling each with chopped parsley and sliced mushrooms. Thicken stock with a little cornflour and add enough to cover ingredients. Cover with pastry, ornament the top with flowers and leaves cut from scraps of pastry, glaze with egg. Bake in hot oven for 20 minutes, then lessen heat and cook 1 hour longer with pastry covered; arrange a pie collar around. Serve hot or cold.

This is a quick and easy pie, as the filling is not pre-cooked and requires few ingredients for a tasty result and tender chicken. The flavour could be varied with additional herbs, such as tarragon or thyme.

From Amie Monro's *The Practical Australian Cookery*, p. 76

The teapot cosy 1916

gouache on cardboard
45.2 × 54.4 cm
Sarjeant Gallery Te Whare
o Rehua, New Zealand
Gift of the Edith
Collier Estate

create form; not to imitate life, but to find an equivalent for life ... to make images which by the clearness of their logical structure, and by their closely knit unity of texture, shall appeal to our disinterested and contemplative imagination with something of the same vividness as the things of actual life appeal to our practical activities. In fact, they aim not at illusion but at reality.[4]

On the back of the success of the post-impressionist exhibitions, Fry established the influential Omega Workshops in the summer of 1913. Located in the heart of Bloomsbury, the enterprise was a cooperative whose program was social as much as artistic: Fry wanted to help artists find gainful employment that utilised their abilities and broadened their activities, to disseminate post-impressionist principles into the wider community, and at the same time put into action his philosophy that art and life are inseparable. The workshops combined a studio with a showroom, and saw the artists meeting with clients and creating a range of objects for the home for sale or by commission. Fabrics and rugs, furniture and ceramics, and even clothes were produced, with the focus on bold, vibrant and predominantly abstract decoration. All work was anonymous and signed with the standard Ω (Omega) set inside a square, a nod to Fry's socialist leanings and his desire for unimpeded experimentation and egalitarianism over individual accolades.

It was Roger Fry's advocacy for the applied arts and crafts, as much as his ideas on colour and form, that most affected and aided McPherson's reassessment of conventional hierarchies in art, and eventually led her to the view that 'the ladder of art lies

*Still life with teapot
and daisies* 1915

oil on cardboard
44.3 × 51.2 cm
Art Gallery of New South Wales
Bequest of W G Preston 1977

flat, not vertical'.[5] Such a position would have been indefensible in Australia until well into the 1920s, and only then in progressive cultural circles. But in the more agile artisitic climate of London it was an exciting prospect, leading McPherson to resolve to go back to art school and once more expand her skill base.

In the meantime, and after a six-month sojourn in Ireland with Reynell during 1914, McPherson began teaching art again in London. She returned to southern Ireland the following year with a group of twenty students for a summer school that extended from March to August. They based themselves at Bonmahon (now Bunmahon), a seaside village that was both picturesque and affordable. Here the students could paint the landscape and sea, as well as from the model in the studio; the choice of location was perhaps also intended to keep them protected from the hostilities of the First World War, which by then had taken hold of Europe. McPherson's painting *Still life with teapot and daisies* (1915) captures a summer afternoon tea on the beach, the table decoratively set with a pink striped tablecloth and freshly picked flowers. A woman and parasol reflected in the teapot show the idyllic coastal scene behind the artist, with no hint of the contemporaneous tensions and horrors. The little group was neither immune nor oblivious, however, with Bonmahon under periodic threat of submarine attack. McPherson and one of her pupils, the New Zealand artist Edith Collier, who had a brother in active service, sent fruit and vegetables to hospitalised soldiers via the British Red Cross and distributed clothes to war-rationed locals. Soon McPherson and Reynell would actively contribute to the war effort by teaching crafts to returned soldiers.

Still life 1915

oil on cardboard
45.5 × 55 cm
Private collection

There was a confluence of circumstances influencing this venture. The example of Fry's Omega Workshops may have been one motivation to train specifically in craft practices, as could McPherson's avid study of decorative arts at the Musée Guimet and the Musée du Louvre in Paris, and at the Victoria and Albert Museum in London. But another mitigating factor arose after an emotional blow. In August 1915 Reynell received the devastating news that her brother Carew had perished at Gallipoli. He was an officer in the Light Horse Regiment and by all reports a born leader and brave man. One of South Australia's oldest families, the Reynells could trace their ancestry as far back as 1191 in England, and were proud of their long record of military service; Carew inherited the familial enthusiasm for serving King and country.[6] Younger brother Rupert was a Rhodes scholar who pursued a career in medicine after his arrival in England. During his own service as part of the British Medical Corps he was involved in an innovative treatment program for shell-shocked soldiers. There was now pressure on Gladys to do more for the war; sister Emily was already a volunteer nurse and Rupert needed specialists in handcrafts to assist his patients with occupational therapy.[7]

Thus persuaded, at the end of 1916 McPherson and Reynell enrolled at the Camberwell School of Arts and Crafts in London to acquire the necessary skills and qualifications in applied arts. Founded in 1898, Camberwell was a relatively new school, but the curriculum had a clear focus on crafts and trades. It was also Roger Fry's alma mater. Taking their classes part-time, the artists learned all the main aspects of ceramics production: wheel throwing, mould making, slip casting, glazing and firing

techniques, and china painting. They probably learned the essentials of printmaking at the college, too, with McPherson completing a number of etchings and drypoints around this time depicting scenes taken from sketches she had made at Bonmahon and also at Bibury during a second summer school she had taught in the Cotswolds. The women added a social service dimension to their return to study by volunteering at a canteen for army and navy personnel in Vauxhall Bridge Road.[8]

Having heard about the artists' latest pursuit Carew Reynell's widow, May, sent them a lump of fire clay from Kangaroo Island off the South Australian coast, where she owned a cottage. The gesture had a startling effect on Gladys. 'It is difficult to describe the exciting thrill which the earthy aroma of this clay occasioned in me', she later wrote. 'I thought then that it would be the most delightful thing on earth to make pots in Australia from virgin clay ... clay that had never before known potters' hands'.[9] A small, crudely thrown jug with an abstract painted design by McPherson was one result of this unusual gift, which she annotated 'For May Reynell, made of SA clay', dated 1917 and signed M.R.M. within a square, in the Omega Workshops style.[10]

After finishing the course at Camberwell McPherson and Reynell moved briefly to Pentewan in Cornwall, a coastal village renowned for its china clay. There they worked at a local pottery studio, refining their throwing and decorating skills before Rupert Reynell made arrangements for his sister and her companion to join him at the Seale-Hayne Military Hospital near Newton Abbot in Devon. Based in a requisitioned agricultural college, it was the only such facility dealing progressively with

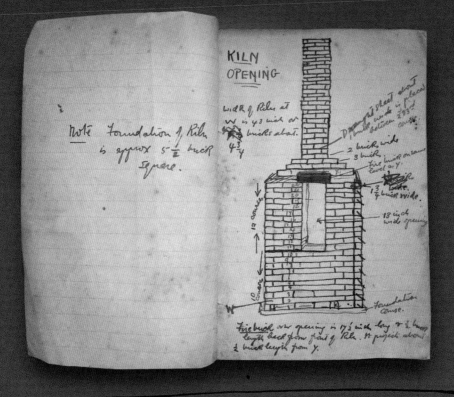

Note Foundation of Kiln
is approx 5½ brick
square.

KILN
OPENING

Width of Kiln at
W is 43 inch or
5 bricks about.
4¾

D iron sheet about
1 inch wide is placed
between 2 9½ course.

2 brick wide
3 brick
fire lump on each
level or Y.

13 inch
½ brick wide.

13 inch
wide opening

12 courses

10 courses

Foundation
course.

Firebrick over opening is 17½ inch long & ½ brick
length back from front of Kiln. It projects about
½ brick length from Y.

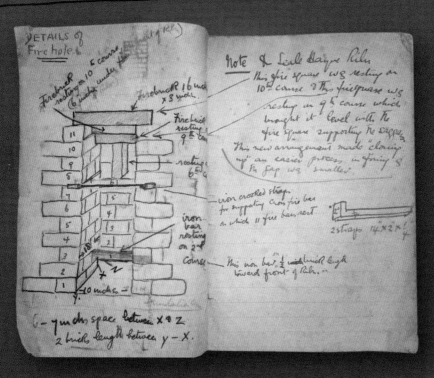

DETAILS of
Fire hole

Firebrick 10 & course
resting on
6 inch under the

(... of Kiln)

Firebrick 16 inch
× 3 inch.

Firebrick
resting on
9th course

resting on
6th course

iron crooked strap

iron
bar
resting
on 2nd
course

10 inches

10 inches

Note & Scale Sagger Kiln
This fire square was resting on
10th course & this firesquare was
resting on 9th course which
brought it level with the
fire square supporting the sagger.
This new arrangement made "closing
up" an easier process, in firing &
the gap was smaller.

iron crooked strap
for supporting cross fire bar
on which 11 fire bars rest

This iron bar, ½ inch thick length
towards front of Kiln.

2 straps 14 × 2 × ½

6 – 7 inches space between X & Z.
2 brick length between y – X.

rehabilitation. Admissions were for 'the rank and file', McPherson noted, and not for officers. Under the strict supervision of the doctors the two artists devised a program of activities to suit the various needs of the soldiers, including basket-making to recover manual mobility and pottery for those suffering from shell-shock—an activity that required mental effort in design and planning as well as offering healing contact with the earth. More seriously damaged servicemen were encouraged to make monotypes, stencils, batiks and other handcrafts that were less taxing.[11]

McPherson and Reynell were inventive and adaptive in their procurement of supplies to run the classes. When stocks of cane ran out at the hospital they used young rose stems, raffia and lucerne, with the amusing result that some of these war baskets sold in the local town started to 'shoot' on shopping expeditions.[12] Similarly, local plants were collected to create fabric dyes, which were cooked up in jam tins—sorrel gave a good yellow, iris bulbs a suitable black—while woodblocks for printing were made on timber cast-offs, from cigar box lids to old pieces of furniture cut down for the task.

Once they established the necessary facilities, the mainstay of their curriculum was pottery. As McPherson noted, it was 'a self made affair from beginning to end'.[13] They set up in the college's former dairy and constructed a kiln with the help of the patients, based on one they had used in Cornwall. A notebook by McPherson contains detailed plans for the structure, including annotated diagrams of the front view, and interior and cross-sections of the various brick courses. Clay was dug from the nearby moors and carried back to the pottery, where the patients

Drawings of kiln construction from McPherson's sketchbook 1917

Margaret Preston papers
Art Gallery of New South Wales

Margaret McPherson and
her dog Little Jim c. 1915

Photographer unknown
Margaret Preston papers
Art Gallery of New South Wales

LAMB CUTLETS A L'ITALIENNE

7 or 9 lamb cutlets

60 g butter

lemon juice

1 dessertspoon parsley

salt and pepper

450 ml Italian sauce

mashed potatoes

green peas

Italian sauce

45 g butter

1 tbsp finely chopped mushroom

1 tbsp finely chopped shallot

1 bay leaf

1 glass sherry

2 dessertspoons tomato sauce

360 ml brown sauce

salt and cayenne pepper

Brown Sauce

30 g butter

1 piece each of carrot, turnip, onion and celery

1 heaped tbsp flour

575 ml stock or water

1 bunch of herbs (eg sage, parsley, bay, oregano, thyme)

6 peppercorns

2 or 3 cloves

1 blade mace

salt and pepper

piece of bacon rind or bone

Prepare and trim the cutlets. Melt half the butter and brush on each side of the cutlets. Grill for 7 to 10 minutes. Mix the remainder of the butter with a good squeeze of lemon juice and chopped parsley, and coat the cutlets thickly with this mixture.

Re-heat the sauce and return the cutlets to the oven for 3 minutes. Serve with a border of mashed potatoes, the peas in the centre and the Italian sauce around it.

ITALIAN SAUCE

Melt the butter, add the mushroom, shallot and bay leaf, and simmer very gently for about half an hour, taking care they do not discolour. Remove the bay leaf, add the sherry and tomato sauce, boil until it is partly reduced, then add the brown sauce. Simmer gently for about 20 minutes, removing the butter as it rises. Season to taste. It is then ready for use.

BROWN SAUCE

Melt the butter and fry the roughly cut vegetables. When nicely browned add flour, and when that is brown add stock or water. Stir until it boils and thickens, then add flavourings. Simmer for 20 minutes, rub through a fine strainer or sieve, remove all fat, reheat and serve.

From Amie Monro's *The Practical Australian Cookery*, pp. 50, 81, 85

(above)
Plate 1917

earthenware
2.7 × 19.1 cm (diam)
National Gallery of Australia
Purchased 1980

(top)
Gladys Reynell
Beaker 1917

earthenware
10.8 × 9 cm (diam)
Art Gallery of
New South Wales
Gift of W G Preston 1967

sieved and refined it for wedging and throwing. Even the wheels were made on site. Primitive but effective, they comprised a circular iron plate atop an iron shaft, requiring one man to turn while the other threw his pot—the turning in itself was a meditative and therapeutic occupation. For those who did not take to wheel-thrown work, simple coiling techniques were encouraged. Borax was used to glaze the ceramics and the kiln was fired once a week. 'The morning the bricked-up door of the kiln was opened saw a scene like a village fair', McPherson reported, with patients and staff turning up in full force to view the results.[14]

McPherson's own pottery made at Camberwell, Pentewan and Newton Abbot is exclusively domestic ware and characterised by the thoughtful integration of form and design. She used a range of finishes to complete her work, including slip trailing (decorating the surface of the pot with a clay and water mixture), sgraffito (scratching a pattern through the slip or underglaze to reveal the clay) and enamel glazes. Several pieces feature Australian themes and motifs, such as the nostalgic *Teapot with boiling billies and gum tree design* (c. 1917) and *Cup and saucer* (1917), which is delicately illustrated with gum blossoms and leaves. One of McPherson's small dishes features a sketch of a Cornish house, while other works, such as *Plate* (1917), with its abstracted floral motif sketchily drawn in mauve and blue, reference the rustic designs of the Omega Workshops.

Both the training at Camberwell and the teaching of handcrafts to debilitated soldiers had a lasting effect on McPherson and Reynell; indeed, it could be argued that these activities shaped their mature philosophical outlooks about the role of

Cup and saucer 1917

earthenware
8 × 15 cm (diam)
Art Gallery of South Australia
South Australian
Government Grant 1987

Teapot with boiling billies and gum tree design c. 1917

earthenware
14.4 × 6.3 cm (diam)
Art Gallery of New South Wales
Gift of W G Preston 1967

WELSH RARE-BIT

toast

225 g cheese

1 tsp mustard

15 g butter

75 ml stout or ale

cayenne pepper

Toast and butter the bread, slice cheese thinly and put into a small saucepan with mustard, butter, stout or ale and cayenne, and stir until melted, without boiling. Spread on toast, then grill for a couple of minutes until golden. Serve very hot.

Enough for 4 pieces of toast

A nostalgic snack, lunch or supper dish, it is perfect with some salad greens. Use a good sourdough and resist the temptation to spread the mixture too thickly.

From Amie Monro's *The Practical Australian Cookery*, p. 90

*never cook a vegetable that needs
soda in an aluminium saucepan*

CHEESE BISCUITS

60 g butter

1 egg

1 cup grated cheese

2 cups plain flour

¾ cup milk

1 good pinch cayenne pepper or smoked paprika

1 tsp salt

1 tsp baking powder

Beat butter to a cream, add the egg, cheese, flour, milk, cayenne or paprika, salt and baking powder. Mix into a firm dough, rolling out several times until very thin. Stamp out with a small round cutter.

Bake in a moderate oven for 20 minutes or until golden, then transfer biscuits to a wire rack to cool. When crisp the biscuits may be eaten with butter or a savoury cheese.

Makes 3 dozen

Any leftover cheese can be used in this recipe, but for best results use a hard, aged cheese such as a sharp cheddar, or a mixture of Parmesan and tasty cheeses. This is a good basic recipe and can be enhanced and varied as desired, such as adding some herbs (thyme and oregano, for example), a little garlic powder, sesame seeds or a teaspoon of mustard. Adding a little grated Parmesan cheese to the tops before baking makes the biscuits extra cheesy.

From Margaret Preston's recipe book

The pottery of Gladys Reynell, SA 1922

oil on cardboard
45 × 52.5 cm
Kerry Stokes Collection

art in society as much as their future professional lives. Reynell returned to Adelaide in 1919, not long after the war ended, to help her family nurse their dying father. She soon set about establishing a pottery studio at Reynella, building her own kiln, working with local clay she dug herself, and creating her now prized utilitarian ware decorated with Australian motifs and modernist patterning. This required a long process of experimentation with superficial clays from creeks and clay pans, as well as deeper deposits from a well at McLaren Vale, but she remained determined to make 'primitive pottery' unspoiled by admixtures. In the ensuing years Reynell made an impressive array of jugs and flower vases, egg cups and fruit bowls, all coloured with slips and embellished with designs that were painted or scratched onto the objects with a pocketknife. The cobalt oxide slip of the Reynella pots gave an intense blue in the final glaze firing, a distinguishing characteristic of the work that is commemorated in McPherson's painting *The pottery of Gladys Reynell, SA* (1922).

McPherson sailed home to Australia a few months after Reynell, but did not join her at the pottery studio as they had planned. Sometime in 1916 she had met an officer in the Australian Imperial Force by the name of William Preston. Although he goes unmentioned in McPherson's extant correspondence, and the true nature of their relationship at that time is unclear, an attraction was surely ignited. Discharged from the army in January 1919, Bill, as friends knew him, was making arrangements to return to Sydney to resume his position as manager of Dalton Brothers, a mercantile firm and importing agency. At the last moment McPherson decided to join him.

William Preston c. 1916
Photographer unknown
National Gallery of Australia

Margaret Preston '29

**MARGARET'S
KITCHEN
CHAPTER 3**

MRM

Margaret Macpherson

By the time they arrived in Sydney on 2 August 1919, Margaret McPherson had accepted William Preston's hand in marriage. It was to signal a turning point in the artist's life, as with this union came not only unconditional love and companionship, but also financial security—Bill worked at an executive level and enjoyed a generous income—and unwavering support for her career. Her new fiancé was, as their friend Leon Gellert, the editor of *Art in Australia*, once put it, the 'all-time dream husband of women artists … the handsome and worshipful Bill seemed to regard it as his national duty to keep his beloved Margaret happy and artistically productive'.[1]

It is interesting to reflect that McPherson's previous long-term and intimate de facto relationships with Davidson and Reynell bore similar traits. In addition to the comforts of affluence, all three partners were intelligent, younger and less outspoken than McPherson, content to fall in with her plans and prioritise her creative endeavours. Davidson had long ago moved on to another relationship with a woman, by now living with her lover Marguerite Le Roy in Paris. Reynell, on the other hand, felt cast adrift by McPherson's engagement after their nine-year association. Bill Preston's comment some forty years later that he 'broke up a twosome'[2] hints at the chagrin and sadness felt by Reynell after the announcement. In fact it precipitated a major falling out between the women.

This was a disappointing state of affairs, not least because McPherson and Reynell had planned to exhibit their European work at Preece's Gallery in Adelaide in September 1919. The show went ahead but neither artist attended the opening

(above) Margaret and William Preston in Mosman c. 1921
National Gallery of Australia

(opposite)
Narcissi c. 1916
woodcut, hand-coloured
47 × 37 cm
Private collection

(previous pages)
For a little girl 1929 (detail), see page 82.

Circular Quay 1920

woodcut, hand-coloured
21.5 × 27.4 cm
National Gallery of Australia
Purchased 2004

RICE SHAPES

½ lb rice

1 pint milk

lemon rind

few drops lemon essence

2 tablespoons sugar

jam

Wash the rice, put into a saucepan with the milk and rind, and cook till tender and all milk is absorbed; add sugar and essence, and pour into a mould. When set, turn onto a glass dish, and decorate with small heaps of jam.

Margaret Preston wrote to Amie Monro at Sydney Technical College, where Monro was then an instructress in domestic science, for clarification on this recipe, as she couldn't get the rice to hold together after several attempts.

Source: Amie Monro's *The Practical Australian Cookery*, p. 124

function, leaving the eminent speaker somewhat curtailed in his ability to interpret the modern work with which he was confronted. The Governor of South Australia, Sir Henry Galway, had been enlisted to launch the exhibition and in his speech he confessed to a personal preference for landscapes over still-life studies, and the refined painting of the old masters over the 'new style'. He did, however, praise the pottery on display, which comprised examples by the two artists and a range of works by the soldiers at Seale-Hayne, observing that craft was not only useful and educational, but it gave the shell-shocked soldiers something to 'draw away their thoughts from the events which had so upset them'.[3]

(Mosman Bay) c. 1920

woodcut, hand-coloured
20.5 × 26.5 cm
Private collection

CHRISTMAS PUDDING

225 g finely
chopped suet

170 g plain flour

170 g fresh
breadcrumbs

225 g brown sugar

1 tsp grated nutmeg

2 tsp mixed spice

225 g currants

225 g raisins

115 g sultanas

225 g chopped peel

grated rind of 1 lemon

salt

115 g almonds

6 eggs

½ cup brandy

Sauce

90 g butter

1 cup sugar

2 eggs

3 tbsp boiling water

½ tsp vanilla essence

2 tbsp wine or brandy

Rub suet into flour, then add breadcrumbs, sugar, spice, fruit, peel, rind, salt and almonds, which have been thoroughly cleaned and dried, and mix well together. Beat eggs well, add them to the brandy, and then stir into other ingredients. When well mixed pour into a well-greased mould, or into a dry-floured pudding cloth. Tie firmly, plunge into boiling water and cook for 4 hours. Care should be taken to keep up the quantity of boiling water and not allow it to go off the boil. Hang in a cool dry place until required.

When required, boil 2 hours longer and serve with custard or Margaret Preston's Christmas pudding sauce.

Butter can be substituted for the suet if preferred or suet is unavailable.

From Amie Monro's *The Practical Australian Cookery*, p. 118

SAUCE

Cream the butter and sugar. Beat the eggs well and add to the butter and sugar. Add boiling water and beat hard again. Add vanilla and wine or brandy, and beat all to a froth just before serving.

Serves 4–6

From Margaret Preston's recipe book

His call for a similar enterprise to be started for returned soldiers in Australia was prescient,[4] as soon the Arts and Crafts societies, the Red Cross and various military hospitals began conducting remedial art classes for returned servicemen. Though the primary aim was therapeutic, there was also the potentiality for discharged servicemen to emerge from such training equipped with sufficient skills to make a future livelihood. The Disabled Soldiers Pottery was established in Sydney in 1921 with this as its aim, followed by equivalent outlets in Melbourne and Brisbane.[5]

The rift between the former confidantes was repaired by the time Margaret Rose McPherson and William George Preston married on the last day of 1919 at Christ Church, O'Halloran Hill, in Adelaide. Gladys and May Reynell were witnesses, and Gladys hosted the reception at Reynella. With Preece's exhibition of the artwork produced in England and Ireland behind her, the newlywed ushered in the next decade with a new identity and a new phase of her career. She had changed her name a couple of times already, exhibiting as Rose McPherson and Margaret Macpherson. 'If I used my new name, and my work was accepted, it would prove whether my work was good, and whether it was worthwhile going on', she surmised.[6] Her goal was achieved in a short space of time. The paintings and prints she created as Margaret Preston in the 1920s have been regarded as a highpoint in her oeuvre, giving rise to her reputation as a leading and highly individual modernist artist.

After a honeymoon on Norfolk and Lord Howe islands the Prestons stayed at Glenorie, a bayside apartment block in Musgrave Street, Mosman, before moving to a house at 11 Park

Corner of Mosman Bay 1929

oil on canvas
52.5 × 45.8 cm
National Gallery of Victoria
Purchased through The Art Foundation of
Victoria with the assistance of Westpac Banking
Corporation, Founder Benefactor 1997

Avenue in the same suburb in 1922, where they would live for the next ten years. There, as Leon Gellert ironically observed, she settled down to 'a quiet married life', which consisted of 'racing madly round the planet with her husband between apoplectic bursts of creative energy'.[7] Margaret had moved continually in the years until her marriage at age forty-four, and although her peripatetic lifestyle continued unabated she did at last put down some roots. While, as Gellert alluded, this would not slow her restless tendencies, now she needed to equip, decorate and create a home. It is regrettable that no visual documentation of her Mosman residence remains, though Harold Cazneaux photographed the artist in her abundant garden there in 1924, and an earlier newspaper article reported on some of the house's ambience:

> Tall gum trees on all sides, bush everywhere, a bridge spanning a great ravine, and then quite suddenly the guest comes upon Preston, the harbourside-home of a famous Sydney woman artist … Here she works and dreams and idealises far from the madding crowd in an atmosphere of her own creating. Not a dull one, but full of the stir of her own vivacious personality.[8]

The writer commended the commonplace subjects of her paintings—'those simple, dear things that, after all, matter so much'— and remarked on Preston's affection for pottery and its making. 'Her love of this cult is expressed in many ways: her own handiwork, lovely china gleaming from shelves, and on a huge wicker chair, with its teapot and platters of blue, that blue of sea and sky and petals of delphinium loved by the lover of Nature'.[9]

Margaret Preston at her
home in Mosman 1924

Photograph: Harold Cazneaux
National Gallery of Australia
Gift of Mrs L Hawkins 1987

BREAD SAUCE TO SERVE
WITH ROAST FOWL

1 onion

1 cup milk

1 clove

1 blade mace

60 g breadcrumbs

60 g butter

salt

cayenne pepper

Peel the onion and put into a saucepan with the milk, clove and mace. Bring slowly to the boil, add the breadcrumbs, then leave by the side of the fire for about 15 minutes or until the bread thickens and becomes soft. Remove the onion and spices, add the butter and seasoning, and beat with a fork. Reheat before serving.

Margaret Preston had a second recipe for this sauce, in which the mace is omitted and the onion is studded with cloves before it is simmered in the milk.

From Margaret Preston's scrapbook

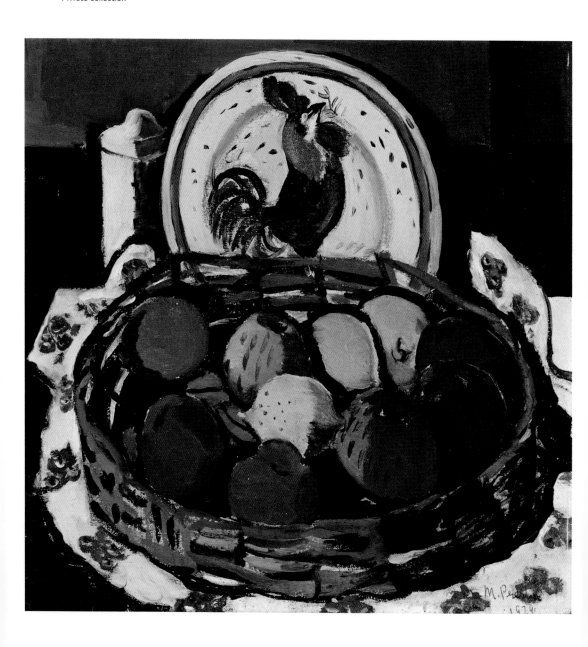

Preston's preferences in décor were typically modern, though any hard lines were softened with rugs, ceramics and pictures she had collected on her travels or made herself, or with objects that held sentimental value. As an artist she was considered an arbiter of taste, and her friendship with Sydney Ure Smith, publisher of *The Home* magazine, saw her publicly opine on modern interior decoration published on a number of occasions.

To that end, when asked to make some practical suggestions on furnishing a bedroom, she recommended pale painted walls in cream or pink, light woodwork with a matt rather than varnished surface, floorboards stained or painted and topped with seagrass mats or grey soft rugs by the bedside, and short curtains in a bright striped and washable fabric. Simple furniture was called for, straight-lined and made of wood and cane. No ornaments, no overhead lights, and only a few intimate possessions such as favourite books and silver and glass dressing-table effects were needed. And strictly no oil paintings in the bedroom, Preston instructed; a watercolour or print was the appropriate option.[10]

When invited to join a panel of experts called upon to denounce those household objects that offended personal taste she was similarly direct, listing 'hat racks with stags' heads or mirrors in the centre. Eccentrically shaped chairs, called "Antiques". Half-moon tables. Wobbly tea tables. Odd pedestals. Heavily carved framed mirrors. Crazy-shaped cushions.'[11] She also lamented the souvenir-style Australiana tradition in home décor: 'may no one ever give me a suede cushion cover worked with a kookaburra, or horrors of misapplied energy in the form of paper-cutters,

Adrian Feint
Bookplate for William
and Margaret Preston 1928

woodcut
Margaret Preston papers
Art Gallery of New South Wales

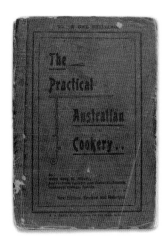

Amie Monro's
The Practical Australian Cookery, 1914 edition

vases, and ash-trays of indiscriminate designs, such as one sees in nearly every shop in Sydney!'[12]

A settled domestic life also meant spending a lot more time in the kitchen, though by her own admission Preston's culinary skills were initially lacking. Never one to admit defeat, she bought a recipe book and taught herself how to cook. She selected *The Practical Australian Cookery* by Amie Monro, who was a domestic science teacher at the Sydney Technical College. The author also contributed recipes to the women's section of the *Sunday Times* each week, no doubt raising her profile and assisting with sales. First published around 1903, *The Practical Australian Cookery* ran to several editions; Preston probably acquired the revised and enlarged version published in 1919. There were a handful of Australian cookery books on the market at this time, and many more British publications, but the appeal of Monro's book was in the breadth of recipes that called for readily available ingredients. This was not gourmet cooking but a useful handbook of basic dishes for everyday use as well as entertaining. It proved helpful that Monro was a local, as Preston had occasion to contact her when first starting out and after having great difficulty achieving success with a rice pudding. 'I boiled that rice on and off for three days trying to make it set, then desperately wrote to the author of the cookery book ... asking what was the matter with her recipe.'[13]

Like many women of her generation Preston kept a hand-written cookbook of favourite and tried and true dishes,[14] the opening page of which contains the amusing reminder: 'Read all recipes through before starting to use'. In addition to the recipes for food

SPONGE CAKE

375 g caster sugar

150 ml water

5 eggs

2 egg yolks, extra

flavouring

250 g plain flour

Dissolve sugar in water and boil one minute. When cool pour onto the eggs. Beat for half an hour with a hand beater or 15 minutes with an electric beater until pale and whipped looking. Add flavouring, then sifted flour and stir quickly with a metal spatula until just mixed. Bake in two prepared 20 cm tins in a moderate oven for 35–40 minutes, then wait 10 minutes before turning out.

This is an easy, never-fail sponge cake that rises well. It has a slightly denser texture than a classic sponge but keeps for a couple of days. The cake could be sandwiched with Margaret Preston's recipes for lemon butter, passionfruit butter or raspberry jam, with icing sugar dusted on top, or filled with whipped cream and iced with her passionfruit icing.

From Amie Monro's *The Practical Australian Cookery*, p. 152

Mosman Bay 1929
oil on canvas
46 × 46 cm
Private collection

her book contains a range of handy hints and homemade remedies, from what type of saucepans to buy (aluminium—but never wash them with soda), how to serve wines, correct etiquette for hosting guests at dinner, and tips for cooking greens, through to instructions for making furniture polish. The dishes themselves range from savoury items to baking, the content typical of the era and predominantly hearty fare. The emphasis on sauces and dressings suggests Preston tended to roast, broil or stew her meat and serve it with an appropriate accompaniment. Clear, white, brown, mustard, horseradish, mint, bread, butter and apple sauces are all included in her cookbook, as are variations on brandy sauce for serving with Christmas pudding, and many salad dressings and mayonnaises. Similarly, there are a surfeit of recipes for icings, fondants, glazes and fillings for cakes—when entertaining Preston often invited guests for afternoon tea—and a range of fruit drinks and punches, aperitifs and cocktails. Once she gained confidence Preston seemed to enjoy cooking, and on more than one occasion declared her hard-earned proficiency. Speaking to *The Sunday Pictorial* in 1930 she confirmed, 'I can ride and sail a boat splendidly—but I can't make dresses—I can't play tennis or golf—but I CAN cook well!'[15]

Not that Margaret did all the cooking at home herself. The Prestons were well assisted on the domestic front by a long-standing and apparently good-natured housekeeper, Myra Worrell, who started working for them in 1922. Worrell was the sitter for Preston's renowned painting *Flapper* (1925), one of only three portraits she completed in the mature phase of her work and a painting of great directness and confidence. The picture has become something of an unofficial icon of the Australian

'New Woman' in an era of great change for the female populace. However, in spite of its bold handling, sophisticated palette and directness of pose and gaze, it is a painting of contradictions. Myra may have the short bobbed haircut and brimmed cloche hat so fashionable of the era, but her dark plaid, almost frumpy woollen dress and blocky full figure seem out of step with the prevailing style. The painting was not well received at the time, and when exhibited in 1928 the *Sydney Morning Herald* critic called it 'harsh and ugly'.[16]

Worrell also posed as a model for Preston's friend Thea Proctor the same year. Proctor had returned to Australia in 1921 after spending the best part of twenty years in London, and took a studio in the Grosvenor building in George Street, Sydney. A social space as much as a workplace, Preston captured the studio's attractive charm in *Thea Proctor's tea party* (1924). Featuring a faïence tea set on a red lacquer tray and complete with a delicious-looking cake, this work, like Preston's painting of Reynell's pottery, is a still-life-as-portrait—as revealing of the person as the objects depicted. Though Proctor's personal style and much admired interior design were chicly modern, her paintings, prints and drawings were often nostalgic in mood. In Proctor's portrait *Myra* (1925) the sitter is plainly the same woman as portrayed in Preston's work; however, Proctor's depiction of her couldn't have been more different. Worrell is dressed in period costume complete with fringed shawl, bonnet and fan, and a circular drawstring purse—the antithesis of the modern flapper.

Myra was shown at a joint exhibition of drawings and prints held by Proctor and Preston at the Grosvenor Galleries in Sydney at

Flapper 1925

oil on canvas
77.3 × 58.5 cm
National Gallery of Australia
Purchased with the
assistance of the Cooma-
Monaro Snowy River Fund 1988

Thea Proctor in
her living room,
Sydney 1920s

Photographer unknown
Fairfax Photos

the end of 1925. Catalogue number one of sixty-five works, it was
the most expensive item in the show, at 21 guineas. It was also at
the centre of a celebrated *contretemps*. The pair had arranged to
invite friends to tea in Proctor's studio after the opening, and as
the painter and gallery director Treania Smith recounted:

> Margaret Preston arrived with a large cake box and
> immediately asked 'Have the Trustees [of the Art Gallery
> of New South Wales] been? If so, what did they buy?'
> and Thea was forced to tell her that they had been but
> they had only bought one of Thea's paintings. At this,
> Margaret Preston threw the cake at Thea, turned and
> re-entered the lift and disappeared like Mephistopheles
> in a puff of smoke![17]

RECIPES FOR FOOD AND ART

Thea Proctor
Myra 1925

pencil on paper
35.2 × 27. 3 cm
Art Gallery of New South Wales
Purchased 1925

For a little girl 1929

oil on canvas
30.5 × 30.5 cm
National Gallery of Australia
Acquired through the Masterpieces
for the Nation Fund 2015 and
De Lambert Largesse Foundation

ICINGS FOR CAKES

Passionfruit icing

Put a teaspoon of butter in a cup of icing sugar and moisten with some warm passionfruit juice. Beat until smooth and spread over cake.

Coconut icing

Mix some icing sugar with milk until it is a nice consistency; flavour with vanilla and spread over cake, then sprinkle thickly with fine, desiccated coconut that has been toasted lightly in the oven.

Raspberry, peach or strawberry icing

A nice icing of a delicate pink colour can be made by first mixing icing sugar with milk, then stirring or beating in a small quantity of good raspberry jam. Peach and strawberry icings can also be made this way.

Rum glacé

Put 340 g icing sugar, 2 tablespoons of tepid water and 1 large tablespoon of rum in a saucepan, and stir over the fire until smooth and warm.

From Margaret Preston's recipe book

Thea Proctor's tea party 1924

oil on canvas on hardboard
55.9 × 45.7 cm
Art Gallery of New South Wales
Purchased 1942

While such a pique was typical of Preston's hot temper, her fury could only have been enhanced by the fact that the subject of the beautifully rendered drawing purchased for the gallery was so close to home.

A matter of weeks later the Prestons departed on a three-month overseas holiday and educational tour, probably providing a welcome distraction and dissipating the tension. 'Travelling is what I like best', she admitted in 1950. 'Washing up and gardening are what I like least. I hate grease, and I hate snails. But I don't allow my work to interfere with my domestic affairs. They are two things apart. I have had a perfectly happy married life, and there is only one person in the world—my Bill! I wouldn't dare travel much further than Pymble without him.'[18] By now, and with Bill's unqualified understanding, Margaret had established the blueprint for her future life. She would paint still-life pictures, usually in her kitchen and composed of flowers she had gathered from her garden or procured nearby, with an arrangement of pots, vases and dishes from her own collection. She would actively seek opportunities to exhibit and promote her work; and she would contribute to Australia's cultural life by writing, teaching and advocating for a range of artistic and aesthetic matters. Finally, she would maintain a stable home base from which to explore the world, sometimes for up to six months at a time, in order to feed her appetite for other cultures and new experiences, and to nourish her ultimate goal, which was to create and inspire a new national art.

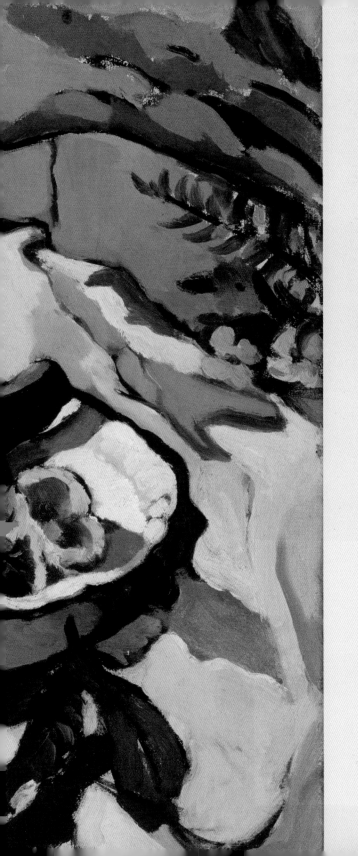

ART BEGINS AT *HOME*
CHAPTER 4

Kookaburras c. 1923
woodcut, hand-coloured
17.1 × 13.6 cm
National Gallery of Victoria
Gift of the Reverend Ian Brown 2008

The sense of steadiness and sanctuary attained on the home front for Preston in the 1920s gave rise to a remarkable period of productivity and achievement. Her art reached new heights as her confidence gathered and her output increased. It therefore remained a point of consternation that while artists admired her paintings and purchased them for their private collections— Adrian Feint, Sydney Ure Smith, Norman Macgeorge and, surprisingly, the reactionary Lionel Lindsay among them—the major galleries were somewhat reticent in supporting her work to the extent to which she believed she deserved. Meanwhile, the unsuspecting public was viewed as 'unthinking' by Thea Proctor (whose friendship was restored) for not rushing to buy Preston's pictures and for preferring the work of artists who 'show no original thought, but always paint the same subject in the same way'.[1] To that end Preston worked hard on raising her profile by giving interviews to the popular press and writing her own articles on matters of art, craft and travel—the last almost constituting a second career.

Margaret's travelogues were a happy by-product of the Prestons' voyages and adventures, which through the 1920s and 1930s covered a dizzying array of destinations, including those off the beaten tourist track. As well as touring extensively through Australia, in 1923 they travelled to New Guinea; the following year they saw Bali, Bangkok and Hong Kong; and in 1925 and into 1926 they explored Southeast Asia on a three-month trip, taking in Thailand, Singapore, Cambodia, Vietnam, Malaysia and Hong Kong, with a short visit to mainland China. They spent six weeks in North Queensland in 1927, and in 1928, after Margaret had been successfully treated for cancer, they took a

(Sketches of kookaburras)
c. 1920

pencil on paper
20 × 16.2 cm
National Gallery of Australia
Gift of Mrs L Hawkins 1987

(previous pages)
Still life 1926 (detail),
see page 108).

CHICKEN KEDGIE

1 whole chicken, or
2 large chicken breasts

1 ½ cups rice

1 very small onion

butter

tomato sauce (passata)

1 cup raisins

3 eggs

Cover the chicken with water and bring to the boil, then simmer until cooked (approximately 1 hour for the whole bird). Remove the chicken and add rice to the stock. Boil until tender, then strain.

Fry the finely chopped onion and rice in a little butter and then add 2 tablespoons of tomato sauce. Fry the raisins in a little butter or a tablespoon of tomato sauce. Boil the eggs hard, chop into very fine pieces and fry in butter and a little tomato sauce. Cut the chicken into small pieces and place in a steamer to reheat.

To serve, cover a dish with the rice and make a well in the centre with a high border around. Place the raisins over the rice border. Pile the chicken in the centre of the dish and pour the egg mixture over the chicken.

Serves 4

Margaret Preston submitted this original recipe to *The Home* magazine's Food Number, published 1 June 1929, describing it as a Chinese dish

(opposite) Skeleton map of the North Island of New Zealand, indicating the Prestons' travels 1937

National Gallery of Australia
Gift to the National Gallery of Australia, through the National Gallery of Australia Foundation 1995

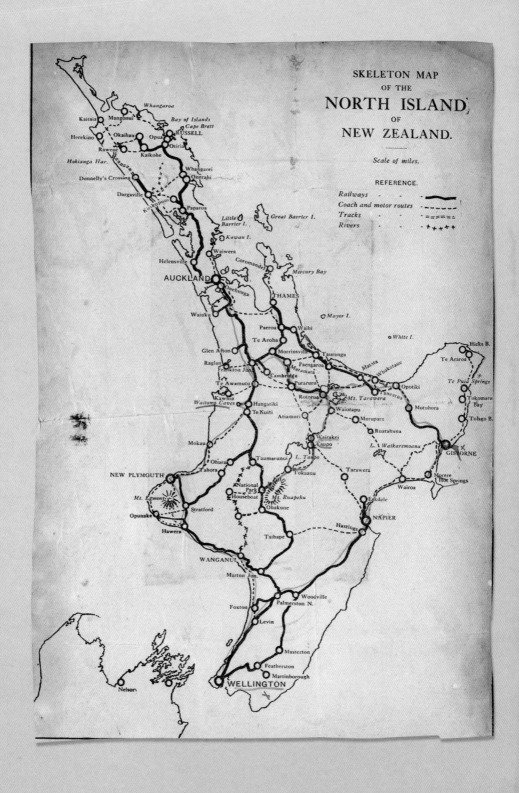

SKELETON MAP
OF THE
NORTH ISLAND
OF
NEW ZEALAND.

Scale of miles.

REFERENCE.

Railways
Coach and motor routes
Tracks
Rivers

relaxing holiday in New Caledonia and New Hebrides to aid her recovery. New Zealand was on the itinerary for 1930, and through that decade, after they moved from Mosman to Berowra, further travels overseas saw them in the Pacific Islands (1933), China, Korea and Japan (1934), and taking a long holiday in North and South America (1937). And so it went on. This wanderlust inspired some twenty articles for publication.

Fortunately for Margaret, Bill was as eager to see the world as she was. It was an easy understanding, with one only so much as giving the other a hint before berths were booked and bags packed. As the journalist Vernon Adams explained following his interview with the couple:

> For both the Harbour has its lure, its subtle, tarry, spicy message of ships from far ports. Mr Preston will come

(above, left) Margaret Preston and unknown person on Stocking Glacier 1937

Photograph: William Preston

(above, right) William Preston 1926

Photographer unknown

(opposite) Margaret Preston and group from the Grace Line arriving in a South American port 1937

Photograph: William Preston

National Gallery of Australia
Gift to the National Gallery of Australia, through the National Gallery of Australia Foundation 1995

11

home and say casually: 'The So-and-So is moored off
Athol. She runs direct to (let us say) Lourenco Marques.'
More words aren't needed, Margaret knows that Bill is
toying with the delicious idea of a trip to Lourenco. Days
later, right out of the air, she may mention a few facts
which she has picked up about East Africa—its dazzling
flowers, its jungles, the overland route to Lake Victoria.
Bill won't charge her with irrelevancy. Her hints dovetail
with his very thoughts.[2]

Margaret Preston
in Angkor 1926

Photograph: William Preston
National Gallery of Australia
Gift to the National Gallery
of Australia, through the
National Gallery of Australia
Foundation 1995

Preston's travel writing certainly added to her visibility in the
public eye; she was predisposed to being in the spotlight and
was armed with a good supply of pithy and quotable comments and complaints, making her an entertaining subject for
interview. But her most effective promotion derived from her
long-standing friendship and professional relationship with the
renowned publisher and impresario Sydney Ure Smith. It would
come to be a mutually beneficial arrangement between the now
mid-career artist and her younger advocate; a recipe for popular
success, as publicity begot publicity, and Preston's art, exhibitions and causes made regular appearances in the media around
the country.

An energetic character, Ure Smith was extremely social, with a
knack for repartee and networking, skills that served him well as
co-director of the successful advertising firm Smith & Julius. As
a young man he moved quickly from his apprenticeship in the
fine arts at Julian Ashton's studio and into a range of cultural
enterprises. Best remembered for his publishing endeavours,
over which he exercised tight editorial control, he was a pioneer

of colour printing in Australia. He produced many influential art books, including Bernard Smith's landmark *Place, Taste and Tradition* (1945) and Donald Friend's *Painter's Journal* (1946), and was the guiding hand behind a number of quality periodicals: *Art in Australia* (1916–42), *The Home* (1920–42) and *Australia National Journal* (1939–47). He was also a trustee of the Art Gallery of New South Wales, a painter and the long-serving president of the Society of Artists, effectively holding a 'benign monopoly' on the visual arts in the 1920s to 1940s.[3]

Ure Smith was interested in modernism insofar as it suited his commercial investment in *haute* design; certainly his own art erred to the imitative and conventional. The more progressive art styles and movements that came out of Europe, such as Expressionism, Constructivism and Cubism, were too extreme for his taste and when he did publish on the vanguard, the articles tended to focus on architecture and the applied arts by the likes of Le Corbusier, Sonia Delaunay and the Bauhaus. 'The modern style is neither effeminate nor prim. But it *is* severe. It *is* stark. It *is* clean. It *is* hygienic. And it is based on fundamental form and colour', he wrote.[4]

Alongside this, Ure Smith was also partisan and contrary: he would happily commission commercial art from the modernists Frank and Margel Hinder, for example, but disapproved of their abstract painting and sculpture. Likewise, he saw no contradiction in simultaneously promoting the work of his old friend, the arch conservative Lionel Lindsay, and a new protégé, the socialist art commentator Bernard Smith. Margaret Preston was one of the few artists to enjoy his unilateral backing and she wrote, illustrated,

ORANGE SUPPER DISH

Peel oranges, remove pith and cut into round slices.
Place in a glass or silver dish, sprinkle with desiccated
coconut and a little sugar. Let it stand about 2 hours.
Just before serving sprinkle on some more coconut.

From *The Home*, 1 August 1929

1 pinch salt
1 " mustard
1 ... Cayenne
1 egg
Juice ½ lemon
½ pint chefol oil -

VOL. 9. NO. 8.   AUGUST 1st, 1928

Registered at the General Post Office, Sydney, for transmission by post as a Newspaper.

The HOME

THE AUSTRALIAN JOURNAL OF QUALITY

Wattle Blossoms—painting by Margaret Preston.

GARDEN NUMBER

OPERA PHOTOGRAPHS AND SOCIAL STUDIES

Price Per Copy **2/-**   PUBLISHED BY ART IN AUSTRALIA LTD.   Annual Subscription **24/-**

Cover for *The Home* August 1928
with Preston's *Wattle* 1928

ART
IN AUSTRALIA
A QUARTERLY MAGAZINE

MARGARET PRESTON NUMBER

THIRD
SERIES   DECEMBER, 1927   NUMBER
TWENTY-TWO

designed covers and was reviewed in each of his influential cultural journals, as well as having two expensive monographs published on her art under Ure Smith's imprints, in 1929 and 1949.

Their first major collaboration came in the form of a special number of *Art in Australia* in 1927, dedicated solely to Preston's work. Along with an abundance of colour plates of her paintings it included two commissioned essays, one by the professor of anthropology at Sydney University, Alfred Radcliffe-Brown, the second by an admiring Thea Proctor. Both were personal friends of the artist. In his introduction to the publication Ure Smith famously commented that Preston was 'the natural enemy of the dull', a portrayal so fitting it has frequently been quoted.[5] Preston contributed a text as well, a curious essay that took the form of an autobiographical exposition. Choosing the rather domestic but nonetheless inspired title 'From Eggs to Electrolux', she wrote it in the third person, a style made famous by James Joyce in his *Portrait of the Artist as a Young Man* (1916); Preston was an admirer.

This way of writing, more recently described as 'autobiografiction', was variously experimented with by a range of modernist writers from Virginia Woolf to Ezra Pound, before being adopted by Gertrude Stein in the 'autobiography' she penned for her lover Alice B Toklas in 1933. When the Dadaist artist Max Ernst drafted his biographical notes in 1962 in this mode, he gave it the tantalising subtitle 'Net of Truth, Net of Lies'—a description that could almost apply to Preston's account. She told her story with an eye to the future and a flexible approach to the facts, a situation not altogether unexpected given that she discreetly

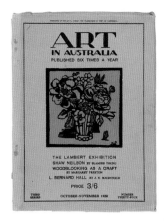

(above) Cover for
Art in Australia October
– November 1930 with
Preston's *Vase of flowers*
c. 1930

(opposite) Cover for *Art in Australia* December 1927 with Preston's *Red bow* 1925

recorded her age as thirty-six, not forty-four, on her marriage certificate in 1919, suggesting she was two years younger than her husband. Importantly, the true nature of her long partnerships with Davidson and Reynell are here neatly avoided. In reality, both relationships had flourished under the liberal conditions that expatriate life offered, but failed to survive the strictures of family expectation back in Adelaide.

Though it throws up as many questions as it answers, the handsome special number of *Art in Australia* was met with favourable responses and Preston was grateful for the opportunity to present her work in this way. A congratulatory letter she received from artist Joseph Connor in Tasmania elicited the reply: '*Art in Australia* is a treasure, I don't know of any other publication like it—the country is fortunate in having Sydney Ure Smith'.[6]

This was followed two years later by a lavish dedicated volume, *Margaret Preston: Recent Paintings*. Running to a small, hand-set edition of 250, it included duplicate copies of twenty-three plates for framing (one can imagine Preston would have been pleased), while the deluxe edition included an original woodblock print. It was expensive to produce and the Prestons quietly tipped in some funds, but Ure Smith optimistically thought it would bring international attention to her work.[7] This was a stretch considering that by December 1929 only sixty copies had sold. The break-even mark was 120,[8] so a full-page advertisement was printed in the 1930 winter edition of *Art in Australia* headlined 'This book is an investment'. At £5/5/- for the deluxe version it was around twice the average price of a print by Preston at the time.

VOL. 10. NO. 6. JUNE 1st, 1929

Registered at the General Post Office, Sydney, for transmission by post as a newspaper.

The HOME

THE AUSTRALIAN JOURNAL OF QUALITY

Cover Design by Margaret Preston

FOOD NUMBER—RARE RECIPES FOR HOUSEWIVES

Price Per Copy **2/-**   PUBLISHED BY ART IN AUSTRALIA LTD·   Annual Subscription **24/-**

Cover for *The Home* July 1929
with Preston's *Lobster* 1929 (untraced)

LOBSTER CREAM

half a lobster

2 hard-boiled eggs

lemon juice

salt and cayenne pepper

1 tbsp butter

285 ml thick
white sauce

2 tsp anchovy sauce

1 tbsp cream

toast or lobster shell
for serving

lemon and parsley
for serving

Take lobster from shell and cut into small pieces. Shell eggs and finely chop whites; put egg whites and yolks in a basin and sprinkle over the lemon juice, salt and cayenne pepper. Put the butter, both sauces and lobster mixture in a saucepan and stir until thoroughly heated. Remove from fire, add cream and fill shell with the mixture. Grate egg yolk over all and serve on a dish with claws around; garnish with lemon and parsley. Serve at once.

From Amie Monro's *The Practical Australian Cookery*, p. 34

When Guests
Come to Dinner,
you should provide—

1.—Soup or Hors d'Œuvres.
2.—Fish or Entrée.
3.—Joint with two vegetables.
4.—Sweet Dish.
5.—Cheese and Biscuits.
6.—Coffee (Dessert optional).

As well as a brief introduction mostly concerned with the disparity between Preston's uniqueness and public appreciation, the book features a list of ninety-two nicely typeset aphorisms in lieu of a summary of the artist's career and achievements to date. Some are hers, others are penned by writers and artists she admired, and a number are less clever than cryptic: 'Be square without being angular'; 'Cubism and nature are only relative'; and, tellingly, 'Knowledge is not truth; truth is temperament; with some people lying is an art with others it is a pastime'. If Preston's intention was to obscure her private life by this means, she was certainly successful. She had plenty of opinions and a genuine desire to educate, influence and effect change, but these rarely translated into real disclosure.

A second, though not quite as opulent, monograph was published in 1949 and was devoted to Preston's monotypes, both in theory and in illustration. Preston certainly welcomed the endorsement of both books and the *Art in Australia* number, but the small print runs meant that friends and colleagues were the primary readers. It was instead to be through the more widely circulated magazine *The Home: The Australian Journal of Quality* that her art moved beyond the rarefied realm of the art world and into Sydney living rooms.

Stylish and aspirational, *The Home* was the workhorse in Ure Smith's publishing enterprise; established in 1920, within a few years it was published monthly to help subsidise the more recherché *Art in Australia*. It was aimed at Australian women with an eye and an appetite for the finer things in life, and its contributors were people of taste and cultivation. The magazine

Still life 1926

oil on canvas
50.8 × 56 cm
Art Gallery of New South Wales
Bequest of Adrian Feint 1972

became a showcase for Ure Smith's favourite artists and designers: Preston, Thea Proctor, Adrian Feint, Roy de Maistre, and Ure Smith's mistress Hera Roberts (Proctor's cousin) among them. Harold Cazneaux was appointed official photographer, while correspondent Tom Cochrane kept the local readership in touch with the activities of Australians in London and Paris, underscoring the journal's currency and cosmopolitanism. It was an important professional outlet for the artists, and conversely these professionals lent Ure Smith's reputation valuable cachet. It could be said that his great skill, if not his legacy, lay in his capacity to identify and give opportunities to a talented group of people.

Preston contributed a number of exceptional covers to *The Home*, including her paintings *Rifle birds* (c. 1928) for the Unknown Australia issue and *Wattle* (1928) for the Garden number, with her *Circular Quay* (1925) woodblock print on the Australia Beautiful edition, the Easter pictorial. Most lavish of all is the cover for the 'Food number—Rare Recipes for Housewives' issue of June 1929, featuring a plump, freshly cooked lobster as the centrepiece. Then, as today, an extravagant dish, it promises a feast of gourmet recipes inside. Comparing this picture to Preston's 1901 still life of the same subject, the extent of her artistic transformation is clear. While the elaborate urn is replaced by a contemporary water jug, the white drapery swapped for a neat checkered cloth and the porcelain bowl for simple rustic pottery, it is the handling that is so thoroughly changed. Preston's objects are still closely observed but reduced to their essential forms, while the picture plane is tipped vertically, allowing the rhythm of the objects to lead the eye around the image. The peeling lemon

depicted in the lower right of the earlier work is now a filled glass that is anchored in the design rather than on the precipice of the real world.

The magazine's usual pages of society gossip and home decorating tips, and advertisements for designer clothes, cosmetics and luxury travel, were accompanied in this issue by a series of articles on the latest trends in food and a host of new dishes for any occasion. Preston submitted a recipe for inclusion, an improbably 'Chinese' (and yet rather tasty) main course she called Chicken Kedgie, which she seems to have invented herself. Having visited China a few years earlier she would have sampled authentic cuisine in Yunnan and Peiping (now Beijing). Adapted to the local palate and using ingredients that were readily available in suburban Sydney, her recipe added a little exoticism to the offerings, and supported the image that Preston

(left)
Flannel flowers c. 1929
woodcut, hand-coloured
24.2 × 26.6 cm
Collection of John McPhee

(right)
Emus 1923
woodcut
16.8 × 12.4 cm
National Gallery of Australia
Purchased from Gallery
admission charges 1984

Bird of paradise 1925

woodcut, hand-coloured
39.7 × 42.6 cm
National Gallery of Australia
Purchased 1961

was not only a gifted artist but also a sophisticated and cultured modern woman.

Cover art was only one way to attract recognition and register Preston's name and style in the public mind, and it was cleverly reinforced. As well as publishing her advice on topics of style and taste, and personal 'pets and prejudices' (Preston loved the Tivoli theatre and loathed 'getting fat'[9]), Ure Smith commissioned the artist to write a number of articles for *The Home* on her favourite topics. The first of these was a neat autobiographical essay in 1923 that served both Ure Smith's vision for the magazine and Preston's artistic credentials, and was therefore appositely titled 'Why I Became a Convert to Modern Art'. Its brief but enticing comments, tracing her progress from porcelain painting as a child to her artistic enlightenment in Europe as a young woman, could scarcely have touched the sides for the curious reader before her treatise, 'Art for Crafts: Aboriginal Art Artfully Applied', appeared the following year. Having divulged the 'bad growing pains' and discomforts attending her transition to modernism in the first missive, she made a leap of faith, acknowledging that Australia had no designs of its own and suggesting Indigenous art was the key to forging an appropriate national decorative art. In one article she appeared as an initiate in modernism; in the next she had found what she wholeheartedly believed was a tidy solution to a problem Australia as yet didn't know she had. This was to be only the beginning of a long and controversial project, and Ure Smith and Leon Gellert as editor played an important role by providing an ongoing forum for what was to become Preston's most passionate cause.

Cover for *The Wentworth Magazine* August 1928 with Preston's *Christmas bells* 1925

When Ure Smith sold *The Home* and *Art in Australia* to John Fairfax and Sons in 1934—a deal spurred by the rising competition between Fairfax and Frank Packer's Consolidated Press titles—the editorial budgets were quickly pared back.[10] The group of designers and contributors who had been buoyed by the original publisher's largess and cross-promotion were gradually replaced so that by the end of 1938, when Ure Smith's involvement was finally phased out, the publications had lost some of their original flair and prestige. Preston then began writing articles for Ure Smith's replacement project, a cultural magazine he called *Australia National Journal* and a forum for art, architecture, design and travel.

Her travelogues constituted some of these contributions but by this point Ure Smith, Preston and a wider number of colleagues associated with the Society of Artists had progressed their ideas about art, design and industry, and were calling for a closer alignment between commerce and the applied arts. An article by R Haughton James in the first issue of the new journal in 1939 lamented the factory aesthetic that arose with industrialism— where the workman was released from the necessity to be an artist and the artist released from the need to make anything useful. Good design 'meets the human and spiritual needs of ordinary men and women', he maintained, and everything must be done 'to demonstrate that good design is for ordinary people in the ordinary things in their own homes'.[11]

Preston's own theory on this subject was less roundly expressed but to all intents and purposes philosophically aligned. Importantly it was born of observation and analysis: she travelled to see the folk arts of other nations, she advocated for an Australian

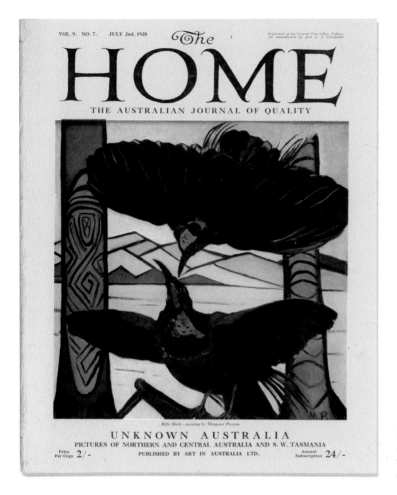

VOL. 9. NO. 7. JULY 2nd, 1928

The
HOME

THE AUSTRALIAN JOURNAL OF QUALITY

Rifle Birds—painting by Margaret Preston.

UNKNOWN AUSTRALIA
PICTURES OF NORTHERN AND CENTRAL AUSTRALIA AND S. W. TASMANIA
Price Per Copy 2/-   PUBLISHED BY ART IN AUSTRALIA LTD.   Annual Subscription 24/-

Cover for *The Home*
July 1928
with Preston's *Rifle birds*
c. 1928 (untraced)

national art, she encouraged the populace to train their eyes and hands by teaching them how to make their own art and crafts, and all the while gave tips and hints to improve the lives and the 'human and spiritual needs' of the general populace. Her position by now was an amalgam of the international Arts and Crafts movement's ethos of social reform—which turned the home into a work of art—and the art in décor example of the Omega Workshops in London, along with the educative approach taken by the Bauhaus in Dessau. By pointing to the 'common citizenship' of all forms of creative work and their interdependence in the modern world, she aimed to reintegrate the artist into the everyday reality.

RECIPES
FOR ART
CHAPTER 5

For Margaret Preston modernism was a set of ideas and practices directly embedded in everyday life, and inextricably connected to her lifelong interest in the applied arts, or crafts as they are more often described. The common factor uniting all the media in which she worked, according to the historian Humphrey McQueen, was 'constant improvisation ... she was confronted with an endless sequence of problems in her daily activities'. Increasingly she had come to view oil painting as a superficial activity and a less technical proposition after it was possible to achieve colour by mixing rather than glazing (an advancement of the nineteenth century). Preston's craftwork 'helped her to realise that it was what lay underneath that mattered'.[1] Over the years she practised the arts of pottery, printmaking (woodblock printing, silkscreens, monotypes and stencils), basket weaving and textile design; all were eminently suited to carrying out at home, a point Preston emphasised time and again in the many 'how-to' articles she published to inspire women in particular to improve their lives by making art.

This ambition is insistently felt in her 1930 article for *Art in Australia*, which extols the virtues of pottery as a profession. With a wood kiln—'no bother' for the potter herself to construct—and access to clay for the digging, the path to becoming a fully-fledged practitioner, she explains in her exposition, is just three main steps away: cleansing, sieving and wedging the clay; making the pot; then undertaking the firing. Though at best a résumé of the craft, Preston's aim was to make potting sound as agreeable and achievable an activity as possible—even if with a small but stern caveat: 'As to the strenuous part of the work, if anyone knows any successful work that is easy, don't

(opposite)
The Spit Bridge c. 1927
woodcut, hand-coloured
27.6 × 19.9 cm
Private collection

(previous pages)
Anemones 1925 (detail),
see page 124.

Wheel flower c. 1929

woodcut, hand-coloured
44.1 × 44.6 cm
Art Gallery of New South Wales
Purchased 1929

FISH CROQUETTES

450 g boiled potatoes

30 g butter

salt and pepper to taste

450 g cooked fish

zest of 1 lemon

1 dessertspoon parsley

2 eggs

plain flour

fresh breadcrumbs

oil for frying

lemon for serving

Mash potatoes well with the butter, salt and freshly ground black pepper. Finely flake the fish, removing bones. Mix both together, add to them lemon zest, finely chopped parsley, and one lightly beaten egg. Form mixture into balls, dust lightly with plain flour, coat with the second beaten egg and roll in breadcrumbs. Refrigerate for at least an hour.

Pan fry croquettes in oil and drain. Serve on a doily and garnish with slices of lemon.

Serves 6 as an entrée, or 4 as a main course served with vegetables or a green leaf salad

Add to the mixture 2 finely sliced spring onions, some finely sliced chilli and/or some finely chopped mint or dill for a more contemporary version of these croquettes.

From Amie Monro's *The Practical Australian Cookery*, p. 19

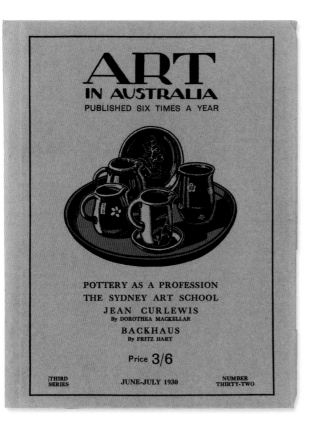

ART
IN AUSTRALIA
PUBLISHED SIX TIMES A YEAR

POTTERY AS A PROFESSION

THE SYDNEY ART SCHOOL

JEAN CURLEWIS
By DOROTHEA MACKELLAR

BACKHAUS
By FRITZ HART

Price **3/6**

THIRD SERIES   JUNE-JULY 1930   NUMBER THIRTY-TWO

1. The ball of clay ready for throwing on to the revolving wheel.

2. The opening of the pot—note the depression at the base of the pot. This is to allow the knuckle of the first finger to draw up the clay—the hands have drying clay on them. The wheel is stationary for the photograph to be taken.

waste time reading this'.[2] Departing from the usual reportage and opinion format of *Art in Australia*, her text is accompanied by photographs of both hand-built and thrown techniques to further illuminate the methods described. Finished works by Australian studio potters complete the lesson, with tableware by Gladys Reynell and her Osrey Pottery of Ballarat, together with Preston's own cheerful teapot and vase.

Preston was also alert to the ceremonial aspect of ceramics and their place in long-held traditions across many cultures, later taking ABC (Australian Broadcasting Corporation) listeners through a history of utensils and pottery. To promote her talk on radio she selected images of women's pots from ancient Egypt, 'primitive' vessels carved by Pacific Islanders, Greek amphorae from the British Museum, Spanish maiolica ware, and modern British designs.[3] In discussing the revival of studio pottery and the backlash against mass production she singled out the 'faultless creations' produced in the studio of the Martin Brothers in England, having viewed fine examples of their salt-glazed stoneware at the Victoria and Albert Museum in London. Aside from the bespoke nature of the pottery, the exquisite surface decoration of Martin ware appealed greatly to Preston, who shared the brothers' great admiration for the woodblock prints of the Japanese masters, Hokusai in particular. The four Martin brothers established their business in Fulham in 1873, each one taking exclusive responsibility for an aspect of the production. But with such specialisation came limitation, and their great distinction became their downfall; when the third brother died the studio closed. Preston was of the view that a good potter must maintain contact with the entire process, from beginning

Cover and article illustrations by Margaret Preston for *Art in Australia* June–July 1930

Anemones 1925

woodcut, hand-coloured
38.1 × 35.7 cm
Art Gallery of New South Wales
Gift of Mrs Alison Brown 1968

CAULIFLOWER AU GRATIN

1 large cauliflower

60 g grated cheese

1 dessertspoon butter

1 dessertspoon plain flour

1 ½ cups milk

salt and pepper to taste

Make the white sauce as follows: melt butter in a saucepan, add flour and mix well. Add milk and stir on fire until it boils and thickens. Simmer for 4 minutes.

Cut the cauliflower into florets and boil gently until just cooked. Grease a pie dish. Put a layer of pieces of cooked cauliflower on bottom of dish, cover with a layer of sauce, sprinkle with cheese, and continue layering, keeping the best pieces of cauliflower for the top. Cover with sauce and lastly grated cheese.

Return to oven to reheat, and brown lightly on top. Garnish with sprigs of cauliflower.

From Margaret Preston's recipe book

Vegetables

Salted water softens lettuces & salads
Borax makes " " crisp & clean

always keep green vegetables boiling hard

Waratahs 1925

woodcut, hand-coloured
42.6 × 30 cm
National Gallery of Australia
Purchased 1976

to end, a practice more in line with the Bauhaus method, in which the artist was trained to complete each stage themselves, from design through execution. Still, the Martins' unyielding commitment to artisan values left an impression on Preston, and she would go on to advocate for the development of a craft or studio pottery industry in Australia. 'Only original work should receive applause in such a young country', she wrote. 'Just get to it, someone, and originate'.[4]

The article inspired at least one conversion. Writing to Selma Heysen in Adelaide, wife of the painter Hans Heysen, Preston passed on the names of two textbooks for pottery (Emile Bourry's *Treatise on Ceramic Industries* from 1901 and *The Potter's Craft* by Charles Binns, published in 1910), and suggested that Selma see Miss Symons, a South Australian potter of experience. 'Pottery is far better fun than painting', she said, but also warned, 'if you help David you will desert your Hans—so beware'.[5]

By contrast, Preston's description of basket weaving was infused with the therapeutic and rehabilitative qualities of the art form. The simplest of all crafts, it was to her mind 'possibly the most useful. It helps the hands that have become stiffened through various causes, it is a very quiet occupation for the nerves, and for the making of simple objects only a few rules have to be remembered'. Moreover, it was a craft of 'feeling' and touch over seeing.[6] Also appealing was the simple equipment required. For non-commercial work only a sharp pocket knife and gardening snips were needed; for commercial work an outlay of around ten shillings would procure a bodkin, pricking knife and basket-maker's iron to draw the weaving closer together. Detailed

CREAMED POTATOES

4 large potatoes

1 dessertspoon flour

1 cup milk

pepper and salt

Peel potatoes, cut into thin slices and put a layer at the bottom of a greased dish. Sprinkle with a little dry flour, pepper and salt. Put on another layer of potatoes and sprinkle flour with etc., continuing until the dish is filled.

Pour the milk over, adding a little more if needed, but also sprinkle more flour as too much milk makes the vegetable sloppy.

Bake in a moderate oven for about an hour, or until the potatoes are tender and the top is golden. Allow to stand for 5 minutes before serving.

Serves 3

From Margaret Preston's recipe book

Don'ts for those who make Salads.

Don't scamp the washing.

Don't use salt in the water.

Don't leave the items in the water too long; when clean, stand them in a sieve.

Don't cut up the salad with a knife; pull the pieces apart.

Don't put the dressing on until the course is near at hand; otherwise the green portions will flag.

instructions with diagrams followed, along with fine examples of work by Preston and artisans of various nationalities, as well as a returned soldier.

Outside painting, Preston's chief interest was printmaking, specifically the 'friendly little craft' of woodblock printing.[7] After having learned the process in England she took it up with great zeal in the 1920s, producing many outstanding works of art. She quickly became expert, preferring to cut along the grain of the wood, print in black and hand-colour her images in the Japanese manner, rather than work with multiple colour blocks. Preston was one of the few Australian modernists to find inspiration in Asian culture; for the majority of artists, ties to Europe and the training available ensured that the western lineage of art remained central to Australian developments. To further her competency and understanding of Japanese printmaking, she and Bill took a trip to Kyoto in 1934, where she studied the techniques of woodcutting with the son of the renowned artist Hiroshige.[8]

Preston also liked to print by hand rather than use a press, noting that 'with work done in this way there is a certain artistic value gained that is lost with any touch of a machine'.[9] The list of tools for the more experienced woodcutter is in keeping with her notion of the 'friendliness' of the art form, and especially appealing: wood of Turkish box, sycamore or cherry, Tasmanian beech or Huon pine, her personal favourite; a three-cornered Japanese knife, gouges and a small wooden hammer; Indian ink or black oil colour; dry watercolour paints with rice water; and squeegees, baren and flat tray for printing.[10]

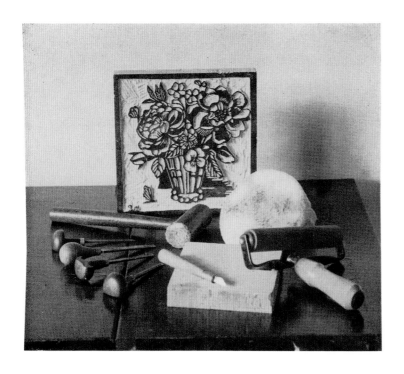

The design of the print was key—the simpler the better in Preston's view. And she emphasised the handmade aspect, seeing wood whittling as an especially satisfying activity that also had great aesthetic rewards, the qualities of which are otherwise lost in commercial propositions. The National Gallery of Australia's splendid catalogue raisonné of Preston's print oeuvre by Roger Butler shows that woodblock prints comprise the greatest proportion of her output, and among the most exquisite. Her *Wheel flower* (c. 1929), *Bird of paradise* (1925), *Red bow* (1925) and *Mosman Bridge* (c. 1927), in which she 'put Sydney's environment through a Japanese sieve',[11] are among the best recognised images not only of Preston's work, but of twentieth-century Australian modernism. Just as the Japanese forged a national and egalitarian art via their *ukiyo-e* prints, Preston thought of her woodblock prints as a democratic creative platform. Thea

(above) Materials used in woodblock printing

Illustrations for Margaret Preston's article in *Art in Australia* October–November 1930

(opposite, top)
Floral, still life (or Blue orchids) 1930
woodcut, hand-coloured
17.8 × 17.6 cm
National Gallery of Australia
Purchased 1925

(opposite, bottom)
Margaret Preston printing, Berowra 1937

Photograph: Frederick Halmarick
Fairfax Photos

Proctor—who was introduced to the medium by her friend in the mid 1920s—commended her for her vision: 'Australia should be grateful to Mrs Preston for having lifted the native flowers of the country from the rut of disgrace into which they had fallen by their mistreatment in art and craft work … Her gay and vivid woodcuts of native flowers, original and beautiful in design, are an ideal wall decoration for the simply furnished house'.[12]

Printmaking offered both inspiration and respite for Preston. The translation of a motif to the clean lines required for wood-cutting ensured she was constantly refining and clarifying her visual ideas for pictures, working out the best way to express them. The manual and procedural aspects of printmaking also seemed to help her broader practice, and even her mental health: 'I find it clears my brain', she explained.[13] When the labour involved in cutting the blocks fatigued her hands Preston made monotypes and stencils, finding them particularly suited to cap-turing the feel and look of Indigenous painting, an aspiration that became especially compelling after her travels through out-back Australia in the 1940s. She also tried screen-printing, seek-ing tuition at the Mosman Art School in 1945,[14] and soon after publishing an overview of the art form in the Society of Artists annual.[15] Once more, materials, instructions and diagrams pro-vide a step-by-step guide to undertaking the art at home, from how to make a screen and what paper to use, to both stencil and freehand methods.

This medium had a further application when Claudio Alcorso, chairman of Silk and Textile Printers Limited, invited Preston to develop a fabric design suitable for furnishings and fashion.

RECIPES FOR FOOD AND ART

14th proof Sydney - Heads - 25   Margaret Preston

Native fuchsia 1925

woodcut, hand-coloured
45 × 28.2 cm
National Gallery of Australia
Purchased 1976

POTATO SALAD

6 new potatoes

1 small white or salad onion

3 hard-boiled eggs

½ tsp salt

1 tsp sugar

1 tsp dry mustard

3 tbsp milk

3 tbsp cream

3 tbsp oil

2 tbsp vinegar

parsley, finely chopped

pepper to taste

Boil the potatoes. Allow to cool, then cut them small. Chop the onion and whites of the hard-boiled eggs very fine. Put the potatoes at the bottom of the dish, layer with onions, then egg whites on top. Cover with dressing and mix gently with two forks. Sprinkle with parsley.

For the dressing, break the egg yolks with the back of a spoon and mix in the salt, sugar and dry mustard. Add the milk and cream, then add the oil very slowly. Add the vinegar very carefully a drop at a time.

This is an easy, old-fashioned potato salad that could be varied by adding some olives or fried bacon just before serving. The dressing could be substituted for a commercial mayonnaise or aioli if desired.

From Margaret Preston's recipe book

Preston was one of thirty-three artists commissioned to create fresh, original patterns with an Australian spirit for the company's new Modernage range, which was intended to bring Australian textile designing up-to-date and make it 'consistent with our times'.[16] Russell Drysdale, James Gleeson, Donald Friend and Jean Bellette were just some of the pool of impressive talent selected. The artists were not paid upfront, but received a royalty per yard, thus sharing the risk—and profit—with the printer.[17]

The discerning Australian public had previously been given the opportunity to buy artisan fabrics, with Michael O'Connell and Frances Burke printing limited-run vendibles in Melbourne in the early 1930s, for instance. Overseas there were a range of more commercially oriented antecedents, such as the artist commissions for fashion designer Poiret's studio in Paris in the early part of the century, and the textiles produced by the Bauhaus in Germany (1919–33). There were other contemporaneous attempts to overhaul the Australian textile industry via the Sydney-based Annan fabrics and the appointment of the Bauhaus-trained émigré artist Gerard Herbst as chief designer for Melbourne firm Prestige Fabrics in 1946. Herbst introduced new designs based on the Australian landscape, though stopped short of Alcorso's model of employing painters. Harnessing the momentum of renewed commercial optimism after the close of the war, Alcorso also tapped into a groundswell of support for art's vital role in postwar construction.

The Modernage artists responded to their brief in a variety of ways, with some working as if creating a painting, and others

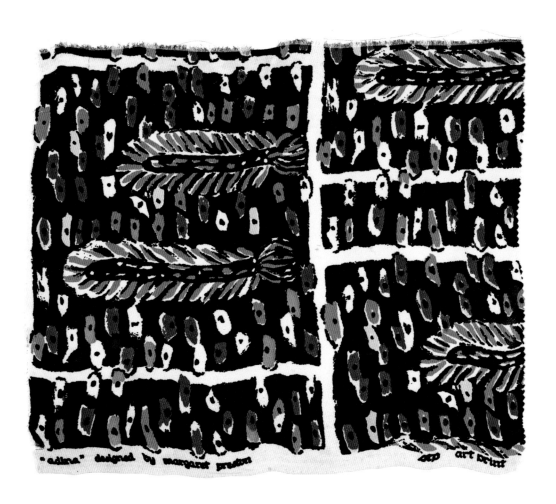

Adina c. 1946

colour screenprint on wool
27 × 40.8 cm
Art Gallery of New South Wales
Gift of Claude Alcorso 1971

conscious of needing to make a pattern that would work in repeat and at length. Preston's contribution, curiously titled 'Adina'—a girl's name with Hebrew origins, meaning delicate or noble—features a native bottlebrush flower against a patterned background in earthy hues. She conceived of seven different colour schemes for the design for printing on fine wool, explaining in Alcorso's catalogue that the pattern evolved from a few shapes seen on the background of a bark painting.[18]

Alcorso launched the range in September 1947 with an exhibition in Sydney at the Hotel Australia, followed by a showing in Melbourne at the Windsor Hotel, before touring it to the United States and Canada. The accompanying book, *A New Approach to Textile Designing by a Group of Australian Artists*, was published by Ure Smith and was amply illustrated with the forty-six designs. While the launch was met with great fanfare and publicity, and the more conventional designs sold well, the initial interest did not translate into healthy sales overall—a result, Alcorso believed, of mistiming rather than misjudgement: 'In the euphoria of the immediate postwar years, I believed, together with many others, that Australia was poised for "a great leap forward" free from the traditional bonds ... However large numbers yearned for the status quo'.[19]

Sydney Ure Smith remarked that the Modernage project was landmark in that it was the first time that Australian artists had been so comprehensively engaged to produce textiles which would rival and surpass imported designs. He also believed, like Preston, that handcrafts and applied arts could introduce creative thought and beauty into the functional items of daily life.[20]

Preston refused to differentiate between the fine arts, crafts and design, and was inclusive of the routine activities of creativity, from cooking and flower arranging to interior decorating, maintaining that the expression of modern life and cultural advancement was in the hands of all Australians, not just a chosen few.

'Not all artists are able to write what they feel', Hal Missingham later remarked; 'Margaret does it unequivocally'.[21] As well as being an outlet for Preston's closely held beliefs, the process of writing her series of instructive texts allowed her to continue teaching, for which she had both flair and enthusiasm, long after she gave up conducting classes in the studio. Even the professional contingent at the Society of Artists was not exempt from a lesson in preparing their supports, grinding their colours, and mixing their mediums and varnishes.[22] Preston was a lifelong student of art herself, and the drive to document and disseminate her understanding of its history and modern applications also saw her carry out a program of lectures and practical demonstrations over the years, at the Society of Arts and Crafts, the Art Gallery of New South Wales, and the postwar Studio of Realist Art, to name a few. Those lectures that have survived in transcript reveal Preston to be a canny synthesiser of great swathes of material, moving her way through centuries, art movements and styles with demonstrable concision, and delivering her summations with the fervour of a missionary. Yet she also recognised that encouragement achieved better results than demands, and she led by example. The great consistency in and connection between her art and domestic life, and her unremitting adherence to the still life as her subject, provided the solid grounding she needed to advocate for change.

THE GENTLE
ART OF
ARRANGING
FLOWERS

CHAPTER 6

Although Preston could hardly have known it when she chose the still life as her preferred type of painting at the National Gallery School in the 1890s, the genre was on the cusp of a major resurgence. From antiquity to the seventeenth century, still life rose periodically from the lowliest rank in painting—under religious and history painting, landscape and portraiture—to a position of greater prominence, as its capacity to represent the interests of the current age ebbed and flowed. Come the late nineteenth century, Cézanne began using this particularly amenable subject to trial and refine his experiments with the formal and spatial aspects of image making, thereby signalling its significance to the development of modernism. Cézanne's pears, oranges and apples, bottles, jugs, and rustic tablecloths were the constituent ingredients for innumerable paintings, in which he arranged and analysed the objects of his own home kitchen and dining table—not to mimic a familiar domesticity, but to visualise it in alternative ways. His compatriot, the artist Maurice Denis, likened Cézanne's process to that of a weaver in the way he assembled colours and forms, and integrated figure and ground, the finished result resembling a Persian carpet or mosaic, or the handcrafts of patchwork, tapestry or cross-stitch.[1]

For Preston this was not a style to be imitated, but instead a manner of thinking that could prompt individual development, though the relationship to applied arts and pattern will have appealed to her sensibility. Similarly, she admired Picasso but did not adapt his cubist inventions for her own ends, as many artists would. Rather, she gathered together a number of precepts demonstrated in his art that made the best sense, and deployed them in her work as guiding principles. She highlighted what

(opposite) Margaret Preston in her garden in Mosman 1922

Photographer unknown
Fairfax Photos

(previous pages)
Still life 1921 (detail),
see page 145.

ALMOND BISCUITS

170 g butter

140 g sugar

1 egg

2 tsp almond essence

250 g plain flour

1 tsp baking powder

blanched almonds
to decorate

Beat butter and sugar to a cream. Add unbeaten egg,
then essence, and lastly flour and baking powder.

Roll mixture into balls and place on a cold, greased
oven slide, leaving a little room for the biscuits to
spread. Press a piece of almond into the centre of each.

Bake in a moderate oven until just golden.

From Margaret Preston's recipe book

3 oz Icing sugar
1 tablespoon boiling water
essence —

method

Still life 1921

oil on cardboard
61.4 × 50 cm
Private collection

she believed to be the most useful ideas of Cubism in an article for the journal *Manuscripts* in 1933:

1 To have a definite geometrical axis.

2 To use perspective as a servant, not as a master. In other words, to use it when and where it is needed, so that, if distortion is necessary to the work it can be used equally as the set rules of perspective.

3 To give objects geometrical shapes in formal relation to each other.

4 To absolutely eliminate all photographic likeness and return to classical form (Michel Angelo).[2]

Unlike those of Cézanne, Picasso's still-life paintings were constructed in the social arena of the café table. Preston's were made in an unashamedly feminine space and emphasised a domestic order, but she also recognised that modern still-life paintings were essentially 'laboratory tables on which aesthetic problems can be isolated'.[3] A consistent subject permitted infinite experiment and variation. The other abiding benefit, she remarked rather prosaically, was that 'you can go on working, even in the kitchen if need be, and seeing to the things of the house, while your work grows. Many of my pictures have been done in the kitchen with one eye on the stew'.[4]

Such an approach and subject matter had its detractors, with one commentator criticising Preston for representing 'the things housewives would rather not see when they go to picture galleries—pudding basins, jam jars, sections of cheese,

CINNAMON DROPS

225 g plain flour

1 tsp baking powder

115 g butter

85 g caster sugar

2 tsp cinnamon

½ tsp grated nutmeg

2 eggs

1 dessertspoon milk

1 dozen almonds, approximately, blanched and split

Sift flour and baking powder, rub in butter lightly; add sugar, cinnamon and nutmeg. Beat eggs well and add to dry ingredients, keeping a little back for glazing. With the aid of a little flour, shape heaped teaspoons of mixture into small balls, rolling lightly in the palms of your hands. Put on greased tins and brush over tops with a little egg. Put a small piece of almond on top of each and bake in a very hot oven 7 to 10 minutes.

Makes 24

From Amie Monro's *The Practical Australian Cookery*, p. 146

method
1 melt butter
2 add flour
3 stir smooth
cook 1 minute over fire

Hibiscus 1925

oil on canvas
50.6 × 45.6 cm
The Wesfarmers Collection

and other not very inspiring articles'.[5] Preston's supporters disagreed, looking beyond the functional motifs in her paintings to a higher purpose. 'We do not think of the furniture and utensils of our kitchens as being in themselves beautiful', wrote Alfred Radcliffe-Brown. 'The artist who can make a beautiful design out of the forms of these things gets rid of the irrelevancy of his subject matter and makes an appeal by qualities of pure design alone.'[6]

Thea Proctor also understood the merit of working with this domestic and intimate iconography, claiming her friend had both an intellectual gift for invention (never repeating herself) and an emotional colour sense that amounted to genius.[7] When it came to choosing her favourite work, however, it comes as no surprise that the aesthete in Proctor identified a flower painting. She nominated Preston's *Hibiscus* (1925), owned by the artist Adrian Feint, as her greatest triumph. In this picture Preston moved beyond the kitchen to present a sumptuous floral display, which Proctor described as an 'exquisite harmony in pinks and reds, relieved by cool notes of green and blue and by touches of velvety black'.[8]

Proctor's attunement to the particularities of hue and colour balance was evident in her own watercolours and prints, and also in her interior design, for which she took corporate and private commissions, at one point even devising a colour scheme for Ford motorcars. Like Preston she was regularly consulted as an arbiter of taste, and in 1924 both artists were commissioned to write an article in tandem for *The Home* on that most genteel but ephemeral of art forms: the gentle art of flower arranging.[9]

(following pages)
Article by Margaret Preston and Thea Proctor, 'The Gentle Art of Flower Arranging', *The Home* June 1924

THE GENTLE ART

DISCUSSED BY

Form and colour. Dahlias and gladioli arranged to form a pattern with broad-bladed grasses. The colours used by Miss Proctor in this design are vermilion, orange, pink and red.

A Thea Proctor arrangement. The blue and white striped Portuguese bowl contains white bouvardias, small rosebuds of white and dark red, orange vermilion balsams and pinky white petunias.

A FLOWER arrangement should be a design. Flowers and leaves should be selected not only for their colour but for their form, and they should be chosen to suit the vase or bowl, the colour scheme of the room, and particularly of the walls. For instance, white flowers make no effect in a room with white walls, though white flowers placed among coloured ones are of value.

I believe it is considered bad taste by some people to mix flowers of different kinds, and even of different colours, though the average Australian woman will now mix flowers of one kind, but of varied colour. But she will have her gum tips mixed with anything and everything for no reason at all. Gum tips should be left in the bush, for they have no decorative value, and are positively ugly in a flower arrangement. The professional florist will mix colours "to tone," to use the shop expression, but will not place strong contrasts of colour—say, orange, magenta, vermilion and blue—in the same arrangement.

From the point of view of the artist, contrast is primarily important. Not only contrast of colour, but contrast of form. Insipid flowers may be made beautiful by introducing into the arrangement some flowers of brilliant colour. A flower of a common pink placed with one of pure vermilion will appear no longer common.

Flowers supplied by Courtesy of Jean and Co.

I N the East, the art of flower arranging is a very old one. Legends ascribe the first flower arrangements to those early Buddhist saints who gathered all the flowers strewn by the storm, and, in their infinite solicitude for all living things, placed them in vessels of water. From

An illustration of what is meant by form in the arrangement of flowers.

The average person does not look for line in anything; in fact, is so unconscious of it that he does not know the contour of his own or his family's features, as every portrait painter unhappily discovers. The artist and the rare person of æsthetic sensibility can see form quite detached from colour, and will select flowers for their shape, just as much as their colour.

—AND MARGARET

such pious beginnings has come to us the gentle art of flower arranging. In a delightful book on this cult by a Japanese artist of the fifteenth century, it says: "A flower arrangement should be treated like a work of art, made subordinate to the total scheme of decoration." Sekishun ordained "that white plum blossom should not be made use of when snow lay in the garden."

Flowers should be arranged to express something. Thus, when you come into a darkened room on a hot Australian day, and gradually discover for yourself a single lovely white flower in a cool silver vase, how much more restful and beautiful than to find a heaped pot of scarlet geraniums, Iceland poppies, etc. A flower arrangement should not be removed from the place for which it was designed. How annoying to sit down to a meal with a pot of flowers designed so high that it controls the table; nicer much to have a low bowl full of the colour demanded by your furnishings, and which keeps its place. Mix your flowers as you do your guests, use due deference to their edges, see how

Here are some flat decorations for the table—the middle pot is blue, Australian made, and has a large pale blue hydrangea in it, and gently dotted in the big flower is some brick red French balsam.

Dark red dahlias with a yellow picotee zinnia, and some herringbone fern, fill a white Louis Quinze jug, whilst little magic zinnias, many hued, keep them company in an Australian piece of pottery from the "Osrey Pottery" of Ballarat. Arranged by Margaret Preston.

OF ARRANGING FLOWERS

THEA PROCTOR

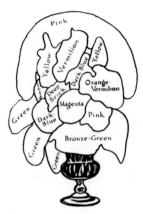

Showing the formal colour arrangement of the flower group opposite.

With graceful forms as a relief, contrast forms that are stiff and severe. With flowers that are round in shape, place flowers with pointed petals. With leaves or grasses that take curves, place green that take straight lines. People who are obliged to buy their flowers are handicapped, for few florists have any interesting green stuff. Maiden-hair fern

and anything else of a fuzzy nature should be barred.

Elegant vases should have elegant flowers. Place simple garden flowers in inexpensive pottery, precious flowers in cut-glass or old china bowls. A Chinese powder-blue or *blanc de chine* vase suggests peonies, tulips, azaleas, dahlias or camellias; inexpensive pottery, zinnias or mixed bunches of gay flowers, snapdragons, carnations, delphiniums, foxgloves and penstemon. For small 18th Century cut glasses and small china bowls, I would choose bouvardias (the large variety), heliotrope, jessamine, freesias, pinks, plumbago, little moss roses of bluish pink—all flowers that are exquisite or small.

FOR the formal arrangement of several colours, the strongest colour note of a flower of especially interesting shape should be centred—not necessarily absolutely in the centre, but near it—and an agreeable pattern made round it of each colour, not making circles round the important flower like a Victorian bouquet, but each colour repeated at irregular intervals in different parts of the arrangement.

I do not like flowers, which were never meant to float, lopped off their stalks and floating in a bowl, though petals and smaller blossoms are charming in a finger bowl.

[Cazneaux Photos.]

A study in pink, white and blue by Thea Proctor. A powder-blue pottery vase containing white, magenta red, and pink and white striped dahlias with pink gladioli.

A study in two reds. Orange vermilion hawthorne berries with other berries of magenta red in a Belgian pottery vase with a grey and blue pattern. Arranged by Thea Proctor.

PRESTON

the sharp herringbone fern demands the picotee zinnia as a complement, and roses, with their frail petals, beg the help of the dancing and frivolous Michaelmas daisy. The Japanese flower book says: "A slender spray of scarlet cherries, in combination with a budding camellia, gives an echo of departing winter, coupled with a prophecy of spring."

WHAT delights you can give and possess with æsthetic combinations of colour—dark red dahlias, a mass of them, and a few of the primrose yellow and pinky kind, all in a deep blue bowl, and scarlet hibiscus with vivid green and black butterflies resting on their exotic petals. How many arrangements in colour, mass and line could be given, but space does not allow.

Here, then, are the last two messages from the flower book: "A solo of flowers is interesting, but in a concerto with painting and sculpture, the combination becomes entrancing. **Sekishun** once placed some water plants in a flat receptacle to suggest the vegetation of

lakes and marshes, and on a wall above he hung a painting by Soami of wild duck flying in the air." And now the last: "That a peony should be bathed by a handsome maiden in a full costume—that a winter plant should be watered by a pale slender monk."

Roses pink and white, with fluttering creamy Michaelmas daisies ... said that a dark table or a heavy coloured cover is needed to keep them from appearing to float on the table.

See how Chinese is the arrangement by Mrs. Preston of scarlet and pink hibiscus with gorgeous green and black butterflies found in our own mandated territory of New Guinea. This could be placed on an oak table or a white damask tablecloth helped with beautiful glass or silver.

For Proctor this was an activity akin to painting—a matter of design, with flowers and leaves selected for their colour and form. She barred maidenhair fern for its fuzzy appearance, and also gum leaves, which she thought should be left in the bush: 'they have no decorative value, and are positively ugly in a flower arrangement', she said. Proctor also emphasised the relationship between flower and vase, advising that readers 'place simple garden flowers in inexpensive pottery, precious flowers in cut-glass or old china bowls'. Thus zinnias, delphiniums, foxgloves and snapdragons were to her mind simpatico with plain or rustic pots, while peonies, tulips and camellias were more suitably arranged in a powder blue or *blanc de chine* vase.

Preston had not yet arrived at her deep appreciation for native flora; however, the careful and sympathetic arranging of flowers had long been an integral part of her creative practice, and the starting point for almost all her still-life paintings and prints. Her commentary in the article made reference to ancient traditions in flower displays, particularly those of the East. 'Legends ascribe the first flower arrangements to those early Buddhist saints who gathered all the flowers strewn by the storm', she wrote, who 'in their infinite solicitude for all living things, placed them in vessels of water'. Taking her cue from the Japanese, she thought flowers should be arranged to express something, and treated like a work of art so as to release their poetic powers: 'The Japanese flower book says: "A slender spray of scarlet cherries, in combination with a budding camellia, gives an echo of departing winter, coupled with a prophecy of spring"'. To Preston's mind, everyone could be an artist, and artistic subjects were readily found in the everyday.

Still life 1925

oil on canvas
50.5 × 50 cm
National Gallery of Australia
Purchased 1980

Decoration, still life 1926

oil on canvas
50.8 × 46.7 cm
Art Gallery of South Australia
Elder Bequest Fund 1940

Harold Cazneaux photographed examples of the artists' designs to accompany the text, including white bouvardias, pink petunias, white and dark red rosebuds, and orange balsams in a striped Portuguese bowl by Proctor, and single zinnias in many colours in a piece of Osrey pottery—Gladys Reynell's second studio pottery venture in Ballarat—prepared by Preston. Such was Preston's flair for flower arranging and the appeal of her harmoniously composed pictures, that in the late 1930s *The Australian Women's Weekly* was able to remark to knowing readers that large bowls of mixed flowers at a society cocktail party were prepared in the 'Margaret Preston manner'.[10]

If Preston's Sydney period marked the commencement of the mature phase of her work, it was by no means the end to her push for change and innovation, an approach which has led to the prevailing view of her art as one of 'constant rearrangement'.[11] In 1923 her desire was 'to try not to duplicate nature, but to endeavour to make my onions etc. obey me, and not me them'.[12] By the mid 1920s she had synthesised the lessons of modernism that interested her, together with principles about design derived from Asian art, and begun to forge her own distinctive practice. Experimentation was key, and Preston never stood still. While in *White and red hibiscus* (1925), for instance, she created an all-over pattern whereby the composition, as in the example of Cézanne, becomes a kind of tapestry and verges towards abstraction, in *Still life* (1925) she effortlessly integrated the separate decorative forms into a compressed picture space— from the curtain and the designs on the vessels, to the anemones and fruit—via the striking black and white striped surrounds of the room itself. Just a year later Preston further challenged herself by abandoning these bold directional bands, as seen in *Decoration, still life* (1926), where she embellished the entire canvas with floral and abstract motifs: on the china, in the vase, on the background cloth and even on the wall behind.

During these years Preston revealed herself to be a talented colourist, though the balance between the intellectual use of colour and the emotive, expressive use was one of constant and delicate tension. Earlier in her career she attempted to manage this by subscribing to scientific and synesthetic colour theories. These became of interest to her while living in England, and a notebook from around 1917 carefully articulates some of the principles in musical terms, illustrating the chromatic scale across a range of variations. For example, a 'Japanese scheme' expressed in C major, has C as ruby red, D as orange (reduced to brown), E as primrose yellow, F sharp as blue-green, G as blue, and so forth. Colours were assigned to the twelve semitones and could also be advanced across a three-octave range. The initial effect saw Preston attributing colour-music titles to several of her paintings around 1918 and 1919, though she later dispensed with this particular strand of enquiry and formulated her own idiosyncratic schema which she evangelised in lectures, demonstrating her methodology with charts and colour wheels, and the analysis of well-known paintings. Gauguin was an important guide, 'a magnificent colourist' following his long study of the Japanese masters, and while she professed to liking the fine colour of Chinese and Persian art, her own conjunctions were based on the solar spectrum of Newton's 'Opticks', which examined the refraction of light. Writing in 1924 she noted that she used about twenty of the primary, binary and complementary

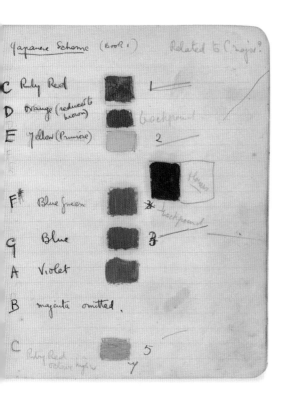

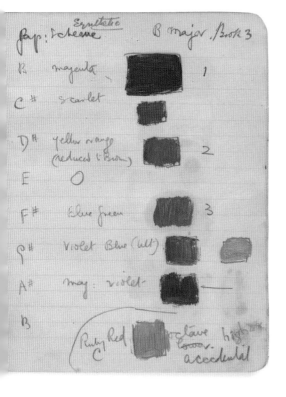

(left, top)

*Japanese scheme, Book 1—
related to C major?* 1920–24
From Sketchbook on colour
theory

pencil and oil paint with
notes in pen and black ink
20 × 16.2 cm
National Gallery of Australia
Gift of Mrs L Hawkins 1987

(left, bottom)

*Japanese scheme, book 3—
B major* 1920–24
From Sketchbook on colour
theory

pencil and oil paint with
notes in pen and black ink
20 × 16.2 cm
National Gallery of Australia
Gift of Mrs L Hawkins 1987

Flowers 1917
oil on cardboard
46 × 54.7 cm
National Gallery of Australia
Purchased 1984

*Western Australian
gum blossom* 1928

oil on canvas
54.6 × 44.5 cm
Art Gallery of New South Wales
Purchased 1978

COCONUT CAKES

140 g butter

140 g caster sugar

2 eggs

3 tbsp milk

280 g flour

1 tsp baking powder

115 g desiccated coconut

zest of 1 lemon

1 tsp vanilla essence

caster sugar for finishing

desiccated coconut for finishing

Beat butter and sugar to a cream. Add well-beaten eggs, then milk, flour and baking powder (sifted), coconut, lemon zest and vanilla. Put small round pieces on well-greased tins, and bake in a hot oven for about 10 minutes.

Make a glaze with 1 tablespoon of caster sugar and 1 tablespoon of boiling water. Brush over cakes and sprinkle a little coconut over them.

These are a delicate and delicious accompaniment to a cup of tea. My daughter Eliza dubbed them 'Coconut moon kisses' due to the pleasing round shape they have once cooked.

From Amie Monro's *The Practical Australian Cookery*, p. 141

deductions via Newton: 'In using them I have never found myself out of harmony with nature'.[13]

In 1927 she dramatically revised and tempered the colour in her work, and introduced a subdued, modern palette, exemplified by the remarkable painting *Implement blue* (1927). Set against stripes of dark and light, this deco or *art moderne* still life owes something to the sharp, perspectival diagonals of Fernand Léger's so-called 'purist' work of the early 1920s, where he combined planes of flat colour, dark lines and heavily shadowed cylindrical forms in a bid to represent modern exigencies and relieve art from the ornamental.[14] As in her paintings *The tea urn (still life)* of c. 1909 and *Still life with teapot and daisies* of 1915, however, the artifice of Preston's inanimate arrangement is interrupted by the real world, which is refracted in the shiny surfaces of the three glass and silver objects. *Implement blue* was hung in the landmark Burdekin House exhibition in 1929, in the gentleman's study designed by Leon Gellert and Adrian Feint. Fittingly for the context, Preston gave the work a title derived from a colour chart for a new line of house paints released by Major Bros. and Co. in Sydney in 1926. The blue is in fact sparingly used, but it is one of a number of tints represented in the painting that seem to be based on the sophisticated palette of the firm's Duralene range.[15]

Other purist-inspired pictures followed, the most imitative of which was *Still life* (1927), now lost but reproduced in the Margaret Preston number of *Art in Australia* the year it was painted. It was a remake, or perhaps more correctly a transformation of Léger's *Nature morte* (1923), now known as *Tray with*

(opposite, top)
Implement blue 1927
oil on canvas
42.5 × 43.5 cm
Art Gallery of New South Wales
Gift of the artist 1960

(opposite, bottom)
Still life 1927
(untraced)
oil on canvas
reproduced in *Art in Australia* December 1927

KISSES

120 g butter

1 cup caster sugar

2 eggs

1 cup flour

½ cup cornflour

1 heaped tsp
baking powder

Cream the butter and sugar; beat the eggs in well.
Sift in the flour, cornflour and baking powder. Drop
teaspoons of dough on a greased baking slide. Bake in
a moderate oven for 8–10 minutes.

When cold, stick together with raspberry jam or icing.

*Also known as 'cockle kisses', these cakey biscuits
look pretty when the tops are dusted with icing sugar.
They are also lovely iced with Margaret Preston's
coconut icing.*

From Margaret Preston's recipe book

Heat lift off fire the sugar & water
Stir in cornflour
Stir all the time when retu

pears, a reproduction of which appeared in the French art magazine *L'Esprit Nouveau* in May 1924.[16] The comparison is so close that it requires little explanation, other than to point out Preston's adjustment of colour from warm to cool, and note the relocation of the image into the feminine domain of the artist's own kitchen. Indeed the objects assembled suggest Preston's next task after painting the picture was to measure and sift the flour, peel the apples and prepare an apple pie. Rather than copying nature, here she was copying an artwork from which she had much to learn, but at the same time feminising and domesticating the image.[17]

The critics were nonplussed by this style of work, believing her message to be 'obscure', with some lamenting that she had 'thrown away' her beautiful colour. Noting the almost monochrome quality of her recent paintings, an Adelaide newspaper reported Preston was trying to express the present era—that of electric cookery, up-to-date tiled kitchens, Kelvinators, vacuum cleaners and the like. 'Now one has to admit that when these things are not white or grey they are apt to be a most distressingly hard pale blue',[18] the writer observed of the new machine-culture after reading Preston's self-consciously written conclusion to 'From Eggs to Electrolux':

> She feels that her art does not suit the times, that her mentality has changed and that her work is not following her mind. She feels that this is a mechanical age—a scientific one—highly civilised and unaesthetic. She knows that the time has come to express her surroundings in her work. All around her in the simple domestic life is machinery—patent ice-chests that need no ice,

Australian coral flowers 1928

oil on canvas
56 × 58 cm
National Gallery of Australia
Gift of Andrew and Wendy Hamlin 1992

COFFEE SPICE CAKE WITH MOCHA FILLING

Cake

½ cup butter, at room temperature

1 cup sugar

2 eggs separated, at room temperature

½ cup strong coffee

2 cups flour

3 tsp baking powder

pinch salt

2 tsp mixed spice

Icing and filling

1 tbsp butter

1 ½ cups icing sugar

1 tbsp cocoa

2 tbsp strong coffee

pinch salt

Cream butter and sugar until light. Add beaten egg yolk, then add coffee slowly. Add half the flour sifted with baking powder, salt and spices. Mix well and add beaten egg whites. Add remainder of flour and mix lightly. Bake in two 20 cm greased cake tins in a moderate oven, approximately 30 minutes. Cool.

Spread each layer of the cake and the top with mocha icing.

To make the icing and filling, cream butter and icing sugar. Add cocoa, coffee and salt, and stir until smooth. If too dry, add more coffee.

The layers could also be sandwiched with whipped cream or a good plum jam, in which case the icing quantity should be halved.

From Margaret Preston's recipe book

FRENCH SCONE OR TEACAKE

1 egg, separated

½ cup caster sugar

½ cup milk

½ tsp vanilla essence

1 cup self-raising flour

1 tbsp melted butter

melted butter, extra

cinnamon and caster sugar to finish

Beat the eggwhite until stiff; gradually whisk in the sugar and then the egg yolk. Stir in the milk and vanilla essence. Stir in the flour and melted butter.

Cook in a greased 20 cm cake tin in a moderate oven for 20 to 25 minutes. While hot brush with extra butter and sprinkle with a mixture of cinnamon and caster sugar.

Serve warm or cold with butter or preserves.

Using ready-to-hand, minimum ingredients, this cake is extremely quick to whip up when friends pop in. It is good with a little butter or jam, but is also lovely on its own.

From Margaret Preston's recipe book

machinery does it; irons heated by invisible heat; washing up machines, electric sweepers, and so on. They all
surround her and influence her mind and, as her mind is
expressed in her work, she has produced 'Still life, 1927'.[19]

It was to be a short-lived diversion, in part because it did little
to advance her more pressing and overarching desire to register a new national art. Preston instead turned to the indigenous
flowers of Australia, which were to be one aspect of her broader
strategy towards this goal, and completed some of her most
successful and beloved paintings. *Banksia* (1927) is a rare and
elegant statement predominantly of white, black and grey, con-
traposed with the eponymous native bloom delicately rendered
and closely studied, and aptly displayed in Gladys Reynell's austere cylindrical vases. *Gum blossom (or eucalyptus)* (1928) has as
its focus not the bursting pink blossoms, as might be expected,
but the undulating rhythm of the plant's characteristic grey-
green leaves, again set against a black and white abstracted
backdrop. By contrast, *Western Australian gum blossom* (1928)
sees the pliable eucalyptus leaves take an architectural role in
the pictorial structure and provide the 'definite axis' promoted
by Picasso. This is an exacting, brave, yet incredibly beautiful
painting, and one of Preston's finest. Together these works are
testimony to her observational skills, her capacity to find order
and geometry in organic forms, and her ability to be modern but
individual—an especially difficult prospect in modernism's age
of influence. In all probability they could not have been made
without the lessons of the 1927 'Electrolux' paintings, but these
pictures, too, represented only a brief foray.

Banksia 1927

oil on canvas on plywood
55.7 × 45.9 cm
National Gallery of Australia
Purchased 1962

Whether deterred by the criticism or by her own cold feet, a return to natural colour and naturalism followed, notwithstanding the harmonious tones of her *Australian gum blossom* (1928) and the vibrant depictions of coral flowers the same year. But these and most of the rest of her paintings of the later 1920s are less bold and more representational, and in the final assessment are overshadowed by the earlier decorative and modernist works. This did not deter and actually may have aided the rise in Preston's popular success at the time, however, which accorded with overdue recognition from the Art Gallery of New South Wales. The decade closed with a self-portrait commission from the gallery, an honour hitherto bestowed upon a long list of establishment and male artists. Having largely given away figure painting since her second spell in Europe in 1912–19, she

Australian gum blossom
1928

oil on canvas
55.5 × 55.5 cm
Art Gallery of New South Wales
Purchased 1928

could see that it provided an excellent opportunity to advance not only her own reputation and position in the art world, but also the cause of women artists.

Needless to say Preston was thrilled by the invitation and rose to the occasion, with the resulting image, finished in 1930, becoming an exemplar of interwar modernism in Australia. It is revealing in a number of ways, though importantly not of Preston's personality. The artist presents herself on this auspicious occasion in a confident, frontal pose, dressed in serious black and with an absence of ornament. The style of her dress and hair, and rather more youthful countenance (she was fifty-five at the time) suggests she referred to Harold Cazneaux's 1924 photographs of her in the garden at Mosman, though the setting itself is a careful construction. She is at home, but outside rather than ensconced in her usual kitchen-studio, the neat bricks reinforcing the notion of a stable and solid personality. Together with a simple pot of native Christmas bells, Preston's tools of trade are her only accessories, and even her signature frizzy red hair is contained, ensuring the emphasis of the picture is on her vocation. 'I am a flower painter—and I am not a flower', she quipped.[20] Preston's friend Hal Missingham, the painter and director of the Art Gallery of New South Wales, was more discerning when he observed, 'In this self-portrait a young girl looks straight out of the canvas, not at us, nor the mirror, but way out into the future'.[21] There is no hint of the notorious quick temper or bossiness for which she was known, and she appears invulnerable. All in all it is accomplished and eminently appropriate, and while recognisably Margaret Preston, it is just as significantly a portrait of a professional woman artist at the peak of her powers.

BEAUTIFUL
BEROWRA

CHAPTER 7

The Prestons' relocation to Berowra in 1932 was to all appearances a bid to return some peace and healing to their lives following Margaret's treatment for cancer in the preceding years.[1] Amid the picturesque southern reaches of the Hawkesbury River and less than 30 miles from Sydney, the locale had been heavily advertised in the 1920s as a holiday resort and health retreat for Sydneysiders to rival the much-loved tourist attraction of the Blue Mountains. It had just 350 residents in 1933,[2] but its position on a promontory between a chain of inland lakes, together with its ancient geographical features, abundant native plant life and mountain air made it an attractive day trip or weekend destination. Bill and Margaret had themselves travelled to 'Beautiful Berowra' a number of times during the 1920s, usually returning home with a basket of snapper packed in salt and fern leaves, and armfuls of waratahs, native rose or white boronia purchased from the local children at the station.[3] The opening of the Sydney Harbour Bridge in 1932 provided motorists with access to the northern region of Sydney and this new convenience may have provided further incentive for the Prestons' move, although that same year Margaret published an article in which she derided the structure as the unfortunate encroachment of Americanism and an example of 'Meccano' ideals.[4]

A clear motivation for the change of scene was the artistic potential of the region's extraordinary natural environment. Preston had by now collected for her library a number of books and magazines by the local artist and wood engraver George Collingridge.[5] Originally from England, Collingridge had a successful career supplying illustrations to journals in Paris and London before migrating to Australia to join the *Illustrated*

(opposite) Distant view of Margaret Preston's house at Berowra 1936

Photograph: Harold Cazneaux
National Gallery of Australia
Purchased 1982

(previous pages)
Monstera deliciosa 1934
(detail), see page 192.

Sydney News. Prior to moving to a large selection on Berowra Creek he was a founding member of the Royal Art Society in Sydney. He also taught at Sydney Technical College and authored a number of publications, among them a manual titled *Form and Colour* (c. 1905) and a book on the district, *Berowra and the Unsolved Mystery of its Amazing Ridge* (1924). Preston may well have known the artist. Like Collingridge she would have the best of two worlds living in Berowra: links to the Sydney art scene and market could be readily maintained, but she would be creatively liberated and socially quarantined in the best possible way, able to live quietly, recuperate and make her art in the 'calm security' of the Australian bush.[6]

Thus resolved the Prestons found a generous acreage in Stewarts Road (now Hillcrest Road) on the side of a hill a mile or so off the main thoroughfare, purchasing the property in February 1932.[7] The Springs, as it was called by previous owners, boasted uninhibited views across the ranges and was bordered by an orange orchard on the south side and Nicholl's Dairy on the east. A turfed driveway edged with rows of native cypress, pink and red bottlebrush, native plum, and eucalyptus led up to a weatherboard bungalow that was Arts and Crafts in style—low-roofed and clean-lined, and shaded by jacarandas.[8] The property took its name from the underground natural springs that provided a plentiful supply of water, and which via a mechanical pump, irrigated the terraced rose garden and lawn in front of the house and the orchard behind. The Prestons moved in around April 1932.

Their first task was to refurbish the existing cottage, which was little more than a simple weekender, to better suit their needs.

Australian rock lily 1933

oil on canvas
45.8 × 50.9 cm
Castlemaine Art Gallery and
Historical Museum, Buda Collection

PEACH AND PASSIONFRUIT JAM

600 g peaches

450 g sugar

juice of ½ lemon

6 passionfruit

Peel peaches and cut into slices, cover with some of the sugar, and leave all night. Next day gently simmer until tender, then add the remaining sugar, lemon juice and passionfruit with some of the seeds strained out. Boil 1½ to 2 hours, or until set. Pour into sterilised jars and cool completely before sealing.

Makes 2 small jars

From Amie Monro's *The Practical Australian Cookery*, p. 185

Method 1 put sugar, jam & water on to boil
moisten arrowroot with water —
stir it in with a wooden spoon
it will then thicken & cook

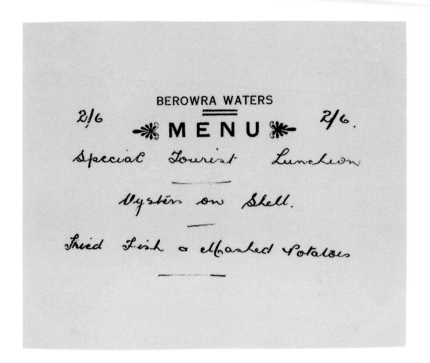

BEROWRA WATERS

2/6   ✳ **M E N U** ✳   2/6.

Special Tourist Luncheon

———

Oysters on Shell.

———

Fried Fish & Mashed Potatoes

——— —

Menu, Riverview
Guest House 1938

In keeping with 'design for living' principles, the Prestons removed a section of the hallway wall and opened it into the lounge, instating a low corner banquette in its place to lend the room a greater sense of airiness and space. They also enhanced the flow between indoor and outdoor areas by extending the verandah, adding an enclosed sleep-out and sewing room.[9] A neighbour was enlisted to build a garage to house Bill's Oldsmobile and a long pergola to shade a flagstone path leading to the fowl runs. Later photographs show the pergola trailed with wisteria and climbing roses, and flanked by a series of small conifers planted in pots on the adjacent lawn. Though the gardens around the house were conventionally landscaped, the Prestons saw to it that exotic cultivars were intermingled with natives, such as the roses and waratahs featured in the front garden. Much of the rest of the acreage was retained as natural bush, though at some time during their residency the couple built a Japanese-style bridge over a little creek to facilitate passage to the less accessible corners of the property.[10]

Everlasting flowers c. 1929

woodcut, hand-coloured
43.2 × 37.6 cm
Art Gallery of New South Wales
Purchased 1964

Calabash Bay, Hawkesbury c. 1939

woodcut, hand-coloured
27 × 27 cm
Art Gallery of New South Wales
Purchased 1964

RASPBERRY JAM

600 g raspberries

600 g caster sugar
(approximately)

Put the fruit into a preserving pan or heavy bottomed saucepan. Bring to the boil, then simmer and skim for 30 minutes. Weigh the cooked fruit, add an equal quantity of sugar, and simmer again for 15 minutes or until cooked. Test by putting a little on a chilled plate and if the surface glazes it is cooked. Pour into sterilised jars and cool completely before sealing.

Any quantity can be used maintaining the same ratio of ingredients.

Makes 2 small jars

From Amie Monro's *The Practical Australian Cookery*, p. 184

RHUBARB JELLY

600 ml water to every
1.8 kg rhubarb stalks

caster sugar

Wash and wipe the stalks, and without paring cut into 5 cm lengths. Put into a preserving pan with the water and boil to a soft pulp (around 15 minutes). Strain through a jelly cloth (see below) and allow to drip. Do not squeeze or press. To every 600 ml of strained juice allow 450 g sugar. Boil mixture rapidly until it jellies (around 10 minutes), removing all scum as it rises. Pour into sterilised jars and cool completely before sealing.

To create the jelly cloth, tie a clean tea towel or cotton cloth to the four legs of an upside down chair. Place a bowl underneath.

The finished jelly is the most beautiful clear crimson and quite delicious. Don't be tempted to prod or fuss with the liquid in the jelly cloth or the mixture will cloud.

From Amie Monro's *The Practical Australian Cookery*, p. 187

For the interior décor Preston exercised both excellent taste and common sense. The furnishings were carried out inexpensively but creatively, with plain linen curtains throughout, walls in pastel shades, felt cushions in various colours and handcrafted rugs.[11] When visiting in late 1936 the photographer Harold Cazneaux and the journalist Nora Cooper of *The Australian Home Beautiful* found the residence well lived in, a 'pleasant rambling affair' tastefully decorated with books, paintings and Chinese vases, revealing Margaret Preston as 'an artist in living as well as painting'.[12] Cazneaux's photographs of the living room show a mix of pottery and folk art collected on the couple's travels, and their favourite pictures: a fan painting by Thea Proctor, Preston's woodblock print *Everlasting daisy* (c. 1929), and her striking painting *Implement blue*. While Bill set up an office in the cottage, the refurbishments did not extend to a dedicated studio for Margaret, who worked instead on the porch, under the trees in the garden—'anywhere the spirit moves me', she said—with her whole environment becoming a place for artistic activity.[13]

The kitchen at The Springs housed a reliable Courtier wood combustion stove and possessed a sense of proper country homeliness, its roomy cupboards filled with homemade jams and preserves, the bounty of the orchard. Groceries were ordered from Foster's General Store, which offered home delivery, and from where 'you could get a horse collar, a tin of stove polish, a drop of ale, a wash board or some iron sheeting for your chookhouse or front verandah'.[14] Berowra also sported kiosks, tearooms and a bakery. It seems likely the Prestons would have enjoyed the occasional meal at the renowned Riverview Guest House, which naturally specialised in fresh seafood.

4/50 proof The Garage   Margaret...

The Garage c. 1932

woodcut, hand-coloured
22.4 × 17.8 cm
Art Gallery of New South Wales
Purchased 1964

A number of friends, including artists and writers, joined the Prestons at Berowra for weekends. Along with intimates such as former student Zoe Castle and her family, the Ure Smiths were regular visitors, and the avant-garde composer Percy Grainger stayed, while the novelist Marjorie Barnard wrote kindly of the attractive home: 'Fourteen acres of ground *au naturel*, a low wide wooden house with plenty of outside inside'.[15] The Prestons also gave beautiful children's parties there, traditional in theme with games and competitions like croquet and pin the tail on the donkey.[16] Bill made the hour-long commute into Sydney each weekday to continue his work at Anthony Hordern's department store—he became a director of the company in March 1938— while Margaret recouped her physical strength and tended the house and garden. Somewhat modestly she recorded her occupation in the 1933 census as 'home duties', though this could also signal her reconciliation with a quieter and more domestic life.

The Prestons engaged a gardener at Berowra, Mr Stinson, and a general handyman, Jack Overton, who despite being only sixteen also took on the role of chauffeur.[17] Housekeeper Myra Worrell relocated along with her employers, living next to the main house in a little cottage that also served as guest accommodation.[18] Worrell's tenure was twelve years in all, only finishing on the occasion of her marriage to local labourer Walter Payne in 1934. Her portrait, *Flapper*, was a wedding present, and when the Prestons left Berowra three years later they gave her an exceptional parting gift by way of thanks for her long service: two hooked rugs in modern designs. Preston had made them herself, one with an abstracted hakea pattern, the other featuring

(left)

Hakea c. 1934

hooked rug
90 × 142 cm
National Gallery of Australia
Purchased 2007

(right)

Eucalyptus c. 1934

hooked rug
90 × 132 cm
National Gallery of Australia
Purchased 2007

eucalyptus leaves and blossoms, which had hitherto been used at the artist's bedside. Both rugs are set on an oval background shape, the designs resembling traditional Aboriginal shields that have been garlanded and embellished. They represent a significant, if controversial, marriage of craft practice and the influence of Indigenous motifs—an idea that Preston had written about as early as 1924.

The nature of these gifts suggests that Worrell's employers regarded her with a good deal of affection, and it was typical of Preston to present something of personal or sentimental value. For instance, some years later upon learning that Gwen O'Regan, her housemaid at the Hotel Mosman, was to be married (to the landlord's nephew), Preston called her back after she had made up her room. 'I'd like to give you something', she said, offering a choice between a saucepan or one of four mono-type prints that were lined up on the floor. Sensing that Preston

FRUIT CRACKNELS

170 g butter

285 g plain flour

155 g sugar

60 g crystallised fruits

1 tsp cinnamon

½ tsp cream of tartar

1 egg

1 egg yolk, extra

60 g crystallised orange slices for decoration

Rub butter into flour. Add sugar, finely chopped fruits, cinnamon and cream of tartar. Beat the egg, put into the middle of the mixture and knead into a firm paste.

Roll onto a floured board and stamp into rounds. Put on a buttered baking sheet, brush with extra egg yolk and decorate with thin slices of crystallised orange. Bake in a moderate oven for 6 to 8 minutes.

This recipe was submitted to the *Australian Women's Weekly* recipe competition in January 1938 by the Prestons' housekeeper at Berowra, Doris Bell. She received a consolation prize of 2/6.

really wanted her to choose a print, the bride-to-be selected a landscape depicting the Hawkesbury Ranges. She later confessed she didn't much like it and would have preferred the cooking ware.[19]

Worrell, on the other hand, was well aware of the significance of Preston's gesture, remarking that 'it meant so much'.[20] The gift serendipitously ensured the rugs' survival and they remain the only extant examples by the artist. Worrell recalled a third rug among the furnishings in the house, one that Preston worked on before the move and depicting the Sydney Harbour Bridge in construction: 'When she came to Berowra, the bridge was finished and she joined up the arches … on one side of the mat only. It was quite clever'.[21] Cazneaux's 1936 photograph of the interior of The Springs shows another modern example.

When Doris Bell replaced Worrell as the Prestons' housekeeper in 1934, the latter's skills were initially missed, as Margaret liked the house to run to a very ordered routine. She lamented to her dealer John Young shortly after, 'I won't be in town for goodness knows when as I'm breaking in new domestics'.[22] Little is known about Bell, though she did leave her mark on culinary history when she entered the *Australian Women's Weekly* recipe competition in January 1938. Her recipe for Fruit Cracknels achieved a consolation prize of 2/6, appearing alongside other delicacies of the era such as Algerian Salad, Spanish Trifle and Ginger Fluff.

Safe in her country haven and with her husband's employment secure, Preston was relatively unaffected by the Great Depression, an uncommon experience for people working in the arts. She did, however, empathise with those out of work who

Monstera deliciosa 1934

oil on canvas
41.1 × 53.4 cm
Bendigo Art Gallery

were forced to camp out in tents and caves in the local district. Despite her tendency to live quite privately at Berowra, she took their cause to the Hornsby Council in an effort to improve living conditions for the unemployed.[23] Preston's self-confidence and sense of fair play also saw her advocating for her fellow artists, using her public profile to advantage by lobbying hard for government, corporate and philanthropic art commissions. Firmly in her sights was the financing of applied arts, which she believed would benefit practitioners and the public alike. It was not an original idea, but a practice she had seen at first hand on her 1937 trip to the Americas, where President Roosevelt's revolutionary 'New Deal' relief program employing artists had impressed her, as had Diego Rivera and Jose Clemente Orozco's mural painting in Mexico. Preston admired the way Rivera and Orozco conflated traditional folk stories, public art and a revolutionary spirit to galvanise the community and forge a contemporary national identity.

The curative characteristics Preston found in the unspoiled environment at Berowra evolved into deep investment over the course of their stay. The virgin bush of their acreage allowed her to enjoy the seasonal flowering of plants in the wild, and her previous attention to colour harmonies and formalism waned. Instead she explored the muted, earthy palette suggested by the plant life of the immediate surrounds and the forms and features of the native plants. Her craftwork and cooking, printmaking and writing, and even her focus on interior décor at The Springs seemed to otherwise fulfil her creative needs, and the paintings she did complete witness a return to a more representational style. Gone are the flattened cubist forms, the singing, saturated

PLUM SAUCE

2.75 kg plums
1.3 kg white sugar
1.7 l vinegar
1 tsp white pepper
1 tsp cayenne pepper
1 dessertspoon salt
1 brown onion
1 tbsp ground ginger

Place all the ingredients in a saucepan, bring to the boil, then simmer until the stones separate from the fruit. Strain through a colander and bottle. Place corks on the bottles when cool. Suitable for blood plums.

Makes 4–5 standard sauce bottles

This sauce is a good consistency and great for using up surplus plums or those not suitable for eating. It does taste quite strongly of cayenne pepper so this could be reduced to taste, or substituted for something milder, such as mixed spice, if preferred.

From Margaret Preston's scrapbook

(opposite) Margaret Preston with the old banksia tree in her garden, Berowra 1936

Photograph: Harold Cazneaux
Reproduced from the original negative
National Library of Australia

colours and the machine-age aesthetic; in their place are detailed and closely studied pictures, and a realist, more 'truthful' vision.

Though she still cut specimens to arrange and paint inside, Preston also began representing the plants in their natural setting—her images of rock lilies a case in point. An old banksia tree in a remote corner of the property was a favourite subject, with an in situ view translated into a woodblock print, while the banksia's flowers were painted in various still lifes back at the house. More than just subject matter, the surrounding bush tuned Preston to the ancient character of the land and was the source of both inspiration and understanding: 'Australian landscape and flora are still in the Stone Age, and their real quality can be truly expressed only by artists who are content to tread the primitive paths of their ancestors, see with their eyes and express what they see with patient sincerity', she explained.[24]

In 1939 the impending war, together with a frightening fire at Berowra Waters that burned for three weeks, prompted the Prestons to review their rural lifestyle. Within months The Springs was sold and they returned to Mosman by the end of the year, moving into a house at 14 Thompson Street—the former home of actress Nellie Stewart. Though she hadn't made images of the Hawkesbury landscape while living in its midst, Preston painted a commemorative picture a few years later, which she rather fondly called *I lived at Berowra* (1941). It was the beginning of another and vital era in her art, in which she created remembered scenes and composite landscape paintings that gave voice to her newfound respect for the vast and timeless country of Australia.

SEARCHING
FOR THE
MAGIC
LANTERN

CHAPTER 8

While the outbreak of World War II brought great anxiety and despair, it also heralded a period of innovation in Australian art. Uncertainty about the future elicited a range of responses from the art community, from the critical documentary painting of the social realists—which was championed by the Communist Party in the major cities—to the angry expressionism of the Heide circle in Melbourne, and the constructivist abstraction of the Crowley–Fizelle School in Sydney. For Preston the war served to hone an already keen nationalist spirit and patriotism, and with the exception of a handful of pictures on the theme, she was determined to go on painting distinctively Australian subjects.

During this time she began her first comprehensive campaign of portraying the landscape. From her memories of the Hawkesbury district she created works such as *Grey day in the ranges* (1942), *Shoalhaven Gorge, New South Wales* (c. 1940), and the sure-handed *Flying over the Shoalhaven River* (1942), the last a tapestry of earthy-toned elements overlaid by a pattern of hovering clouds. Here the river winds its way through the centre of Preston's composition with a determined resilience, albeit with none of the lyrical beauty for which it is renowned and which Arthur Streeton celebrated in his painting *The purple noon's transparent might* (1896). A decisively modernist landscape in its succinct and abstracted treatment, *Flying over the Shoalhaven River* presents, as the art historian and curator Deborah Edwards observes, 'a conception of a place and its essence'.[1]

This new kind of painting was an expression of a larger and carefully planned program in Preston's art practice, though its

(opposite)
Shoalhaven Gorge, New South Wales c. 1940
oil and gouache on canvas
53.7 × 45.8 cm
National Gallery of Victoria
Purchased with funds donated from the Estate of Dr Donald Wright 2008

(previous pages)
Flying over the Shoalhaven River 1942 (detail), see page 204.

mature form had only been reached after a considerable period of trial and experimentation. She had a long-held, if wishfully optimistic goal to develop an art that truly represented Australia. 'Art is the tangible symbol of the spirit of a country', she wrote in 1927. 'What is Australia going to offer to the world as her contribution to the arts? A magic lantern has given America a place amongst the great nations ... What is to be the form of *our* national Art?'[2] The cultivation of a national aesthetic, she believed, required a return to fundamental principles; artists needed to go back to 'the source' for answers and inspiration. This source was the spirit of the country and the fundamentals of nature, together with the efficiencies and wisdoms found in Aboriginal art. Preston was influenced by Roger Fry and Clive Bell on this count, who saw tribal and so-called 'primitive' art as sincere and natural, free from the constraints of descriptive qualities and capable of evoking greater emotional intensity.

While her responses to and understanding of Aboriginal art became better informed and more sophisticated over time, Preston's early public statements about the influential role it could play in Australian society, in articles for *The Home* in 1924 and *Art in Australia* in 1925,[3] were slanted entirely towards its formal and aesthetic qualities, with scant regard for the ceremonial, symbolic or sacred. 'Mythology and religious symbolism do not matter to the artist, only to the anthropologist', the artist asserted.[4] The tendency to abstraction and natural rhythm in Aboriginal paintings, Preston felt, lent themselves pertinently to decorative repetitions in the applied arts. Similarly, the flat colour and the reduced and quintessentially Australian palette of reds and ochres, and tones drawn directly from the native

environment, were held up for their ready adaptation to modern domestic life.

Drawing her readers' attention to a range of suitable motifs she had seen on her travels and in museums, Preston devised a series of possibilities for 'national designs'. The geometric patterns of dancing boards from the Kimberley, shields from North Queensland, totem boards from Central Australia and taphoglyphs (carved trees associated with Indigenous mortuary practices) from New South Wales could inspire designs for textiles, mats and cushions, bookplates, and hand-painted china, she suggested. Copying was discouraged—'That kind of pseudo-work leads to a dead-end or side track'[5]—but close study was supported. The lynchpin was an association with real life and everyday objects. 'Away with poker-worked kookaburras and gumleaves!' she implored, 'it is high time we started to make our homes more Australian in atmosphere'.[6] Functionalism and craftsmanship were the fundamentals of her program, which bore the catchcry 'Be Aboriginal':

> We have teachers and wonderful prints to help us and the rest *must* come from ourselves, and the beginning should come from the home and domestic arts. This is the reason that I have studied the aboriginals' art and have applied their designs to the simple things of life, hoping that the craftsman will succeed where, until now, the artist has certainly failed.[7]

It was a tidy but reductive methodology, appropriative rather than respectful, and though Preston's intentions were good and better researched than they appear at first impression, there is

Flying over the Shoalhaven River 1942

oil on canvas
50.6 × 50.6 cm
National Gallery of Australia
Purchased 1973

APRICOT GATEAU

800 g tin apricots

30 g gelatine

3 tbsp sugar

almonds

Strain syrup from fruit, add sufficient water to make 720 ml and soak gelatine in it. Add sugar and stir over fire until gelatine is dissolved and it boils.

Blanch almonds and chop them up; arrange fruit in a wet mould or bowl, and sprinkle over the almonds. Strain the syrup over the top and allow it to set. Turn out and serve with cream.

Fresh apricots may be used in the same way, but must be cooked in syrup until tender.

This is a very easy dessert and especially good with home-stewed apricots in place of tinned, or indeed other stewed fruits. Piping cream around the edge would provide an authentic, period touch. The gateau can be served straight from the bowl if a mould is not used.

From Amie Monro's *The Practical Australian Cookery*, p. 127

LEMON CHEESE

225 g sugar

110 g butter

4 egg yolks

3 egg whites, extra

juice of 2 large lemons

Beat all ingredients together well and put into an enamel saucepan, stirring constantly over the fire until it thickens.

This can be used to fill a pastry case as a lemon dessert, or small individual pastry cups for afternoon tea.

From Margaret Preston's recipe book

Aboriginal landscape 1941

oil on canvas
40 × 52 cm
Art Gallery of South Australia
D & J T Mortlock Bequest Fund 1982

no doubting that they do not hold up today as in any way acceptable. In its original incarnation her theory was a misconstrued interpretation of the approach of Picasso, Braque and the School of Paris artists, who in the first decades of the twentieth century looked to traditional African and Oceanic art as a model for alternative ways of representing the world. They believed these sacred art forms possessed a raw and vitalising force that could inform and invigorate their quest to define modern life. Close observation of non-western art helped to shift artists' reliance on naturalism, opening up the possibilities of abstraction. This was a reality more conceptual than visual: 'I paint things as I think them, not as I see them', Picasso said.[8]

As well as including mask-like faces in their early paintings, the cubists developed composite, cumulative shapes that responded directly to the capacity of 'primitive' art to combine many forms into one. Space was treated without regard for perspective, concave could stand for convex, a solid could represent a void, and objects might be represented from a variety of viewpoints at once. In short, the conventions of western painting were thrown up in the air. By contrast, Preston's approach was a surface or aesthetic primitivism, which she tested on handcrafts and the intimate and domestic objects of the home.

It should not go unsaid that Preston came to revere Indigenous art and believed it to be the most genuine of human expressions. She and Bill travelled widely to look at Aboriginal art in situ, taking trips through Western Australia, Queensland and the Northern Territory to visit rock art sites and collect specimens of wildflowers. They also visited Aboriginal reserves

*Blue Mountains
theme* 1941

oil on canvas
50.7 × 51.3 cm
Shepparton Art Gallery
Purchased with the aid of
Caltex–Victorian State
Government Art Fund
and the Shepparton
City Council 1978

and missions, access to which Bill negotiated; he enjoyed their adventures provided they had a purpose. 'He likes an objective when he drives', Preston reported. 'A search for some rare flower is a fine objective'. In 1947 they drove themselves from Sydney to Darwin in a utility—a 10 000 mile, six-month trip—on a search for Aboriginal carvings, new species of wildflowers, the formations of the 'forbidden city' of the north and the 'flying lights' of the desert. They camped out, spreading sleeping bags under the canopy of a suitable tree and picking up supplies at stations along the way, with Margaret inventively cooking many a roast of beef on a shovel over the fire.[9]

Preston also studied Indigenous art at the Australian Museum in Sydney and explored the rock art of the Hawkesbury region when living there, especially in what is now known as the Muogamarra Sanctuary established by the pioneering conservationist John Tipper. Soon after returning to Sydney from Berowra she and Bill joined the Anthropological Society of New South Wales (established in 1928), becoming actively involved in documentation projects and lobbying for the protection of Aboriginal rock carvings.[10] It was a time of much change in anthropology, as the field was shifting away from ethnographic and evolutionary emphases and towards a more scientific approach. Preston counted some of Australia's most esteemed anthropologists among her friends, including the British academic Alfred Radcliffe-Brown and his successor as the chair of anthropology at the University of Sydney, Adolphus Elkin, a prominent campaigner for social justice for Aboriginal peoples. Similarly, Frederick McCarthy of the Australian Museum, an anthropologist-curator, became a personal friend and guide.

Designs based on
Aboriginal shields

Reproduced in *Art in
Australia* March 1925

While Preston may have been an early exponent, she was not
alone in promoting the adaptation of Aboriginal art to modern
art and design, with the Arts and Crafts societies of New South
Wales and Victoria inviting lectures on the theme, and public
and commercial institutions mounting relevant exhibitions. The
Anthropological Society held the exhibition *Primitive Arts and
Crafts* in 1934, and Preston was on the organising committee for
the *Exhibition of Australian Aboriginal Art and its Application*
held at David Jones Gallery in August 1941. Sydney Ure
Smith also rallied to the cause, publishing articles by Preston,
McCarthy and Ursula McConnel, a research assistant of Elkin's.

The latter wrote specifically and at length on inspiration and design in Aboriginal art for *Art in Australia* in 1935. Having worked on documenting and photographing the art herself, she was able to explain the meanings of various motifs, most of which were derived from objects that were an intimate part of daily life. Such imagery included the *ká:ndo:r*, a tree from which a cure for stinging nettle is obtained, or the pods and seeds from the *dyúngai* which are ground up for flour, illustrating the point that Aboriginal art was inseparable from social and cultural values and customs.

Over the ensuing years Preston became increasingly concerned with authenticity in art and all that inferred: essential elements, truth, unity and even universality. She also recognised that Indigenous Australians paint and draw 'with knowledge from the mind more than with mere visual perception'.[11] This would trigger the recognition that a national art cannot be 'made'; rather 'it must come from the subconscious and express the national characteristics and temperament'.[12]

Preston's project saw her becoming involved in new cultural ventures through the 1940s. Though the modernist Margaret Preston was an unlikely candidate for Sydney's Studio of Realist Art (SORA), the cultural activist Margaret Preston was a natural fit. SORA's mission was to bring art to the people and encourage artists to become 'an accepted and essential factor in our Australian life'.[13] The studio opened in March 1945 in a Sussex Street basement, and membership was just £1 per year to access a range of art classes, a Friday night sketch club, a library of books and a program of lectures and discussions. Preston, like

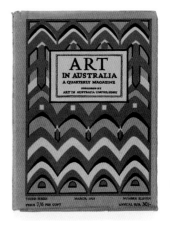

Cover for *Art in Australia* March 1925 designed by Margaret Preston

(top) Margaret and
William Preston in the
Northern Territory 1947

Photographer unknown
Margaret Preston papers
Art Gallery of New South Wales

(bottom) Margaret Preston
with gum blossoms, Oenpelli,
Northern Territory 1947

Photographer unknown
Margaret Preston papers
Art Gallery of New South Wales

ORANGE ICE CREAM

6 oranges

sugar lumps

3 lemons

340 g sugar

1 l boiled custard or
cream

Rub off the zest of two or three oranges on some
lumps of sugar. Squeeze out the juice of the oranges
and lemons, and strain over the flavoured sugar. Add
the remainder of the sugar and stir to dissolve.
Add the custard or cream, then freeze.

*This method of removing the zest from the orange
rind makes the flavour of the finished ice cream very
intense and gives it a smooth texture, and is definitely
worth the effort involved.*

From Margaret Preston's recipe book

Spit Junction 1954

Photographer unknown
Mosman Library Service

RECIPES FOR FOOD AND ART

respected artists Russell Drysdale and James Cant, lent an air of seriousness and experience to the undertaking. At the heart of the enterprise was a desire to encourage art that has something to say and reveals the relationship between the artist and the society of which they are a part. Preston donated seventy copies of *The Studio* art magazine to the library, and lectured on 'The basis of an art for Australia' among other topics, as well as exhibiting under its banner.

Her involvement with the Jindyworobak movement was a similar alignment of sentiments. A literary group formed in Adelaide in 1937, the Jindyworobaks asserted the need for distinctively Australian cultural values derived from the age-old land and its inhabitants. 'The choking weeds of Austr*alien*ism must be uprooted from our schools, and in their place the seeds of the new culture must be sown', wrote proponent Kenneth Gifford.[14] Preston befriended the Jindyworobak poet Ian Mudie, corresponding with him through the 1940s and producing cover designs, illustrations and sympathetic articles on Australian painting for the group's publications. Like Preston the group later came under criticism for selectively choosing and adopting words and symbols derived from Indigenous cultures but applying them inappropriately. Caught up in their aspirations for national anthems they overlooked the politics and implications of their adaptations.

In June 1945 the Prestons moved into the Hotel Mosman and would live there for the next seven years. By now Bill was a director of Tooheys Limited and the hotel was part of the company's portfolio of assets; his position ensured the best of service. The

Cover by Margaret Preston for *The Australian Dream* by Ian Mudie 1943

National Gallery of Australia Research Library

CHOCOLATE TART

225 g shortcrust pastry

45 g butter

30 g flour

250 ml milk

2 eggs

60 g grated chocolate

30 g sugar

Make the pastry and roll it out, grease a pie dish and line with pastry. Prick the centre with a fork to prevent it rising, ornament edge and glaze it with egg. Bake in a hot oven for 15 minutes.

To make the chocolate mixture, melt butter and remove from fire. Add flour and beat until free from lumps, then cook 2 minutes. Add milk and stir until boiling, then add chocolate, sugar and yolks of eggs; cook without boiling. When cool, pour into pastry and ornament with whites of eggs that have been stiffly beaten and sweetened to taste (with around ½ cup of caster sugar). Return to oven to set whites and slightly brown.

Allow filling to set a few hours before serving.

This tart is a real crowd-pleaser that is rich and flavoursome. The meringue on top could be substituted with cream and strawberries for a less sweet version.

From Amie Monro's *The Practical Australian Cookery*, p. 122

The brown pot 1940

oil on canvas
51.0 × 45.8 cm
Art Gallery of New South Wales
Purchased 1942

hotel was well located at Spit Junction, and was both modern and comfortable. The couple occupied two rooms on the first floor, the second of which Margaret used as a studio, and without either living room or kitchen they ate all their meals in the hotel dining room. With rationing still in place in the period following the end of the war Margaret would pinch extra butter and sugar from the hotel dining room.[15] When she wrote to invite Lionel Lindsay to the hotel for lunch she remarked that the food was good, which was just as well, as she 'enjoyed her tucker'.[16]

With the suite serviced regularly, Preston was now liberated from housework and cooking at age seventy (Bill was sixty-four when they moved and still working), and she was able to focus entirely on her work and travel. She was, by all accounts, delighted with this situation. Her friend Dorothy Dundas recalled that Bill was 'always happy with whatever arrangements she wanted. He never contradicted any of her enthusiasms, but I couldn't help thinking: poor old darling, he must miss having a home'.[17] As ever, Margaret's requirements and wishes remained a priority in the marriage. When a journalist asked, 'And you a painter of flowers living in a hotel: don't you want a garden?' Preston, having had her hands in the dirt for so many years, replied emphatically: 'I loathe gardening. I let God make the flowers. I paint them. Here with no house worries I get time to paint'.[18] However, they would make one final move, in 1952, to 22 Killarney Street, Mosman, overlooking the picturesque Quaker Hat Bay.

The following year, at nearly eighty years of age, Preston held what she vowed would be 'my last exhibition before the pearly gates'.[19] It comprised twenty-nine works, predominantly colour

COFFEE ICE CREAM

2 tbsp coffee

300 ml water

85 g caster sugar

1 tbsp cornflour

300 ml milk

600 ml cream

Put the coffee in a muslin bag, place it in a pot and pour over 300 ml of boiling water. Place it on the heat until it almost boils again. Strain into a bowl, add the sugar and stir until dissolved. Thicken with cornflour blended with a little cold water, mix with the milk and cream, and when quite cold, freeze.

From Margaret Preston's recipe book

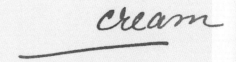

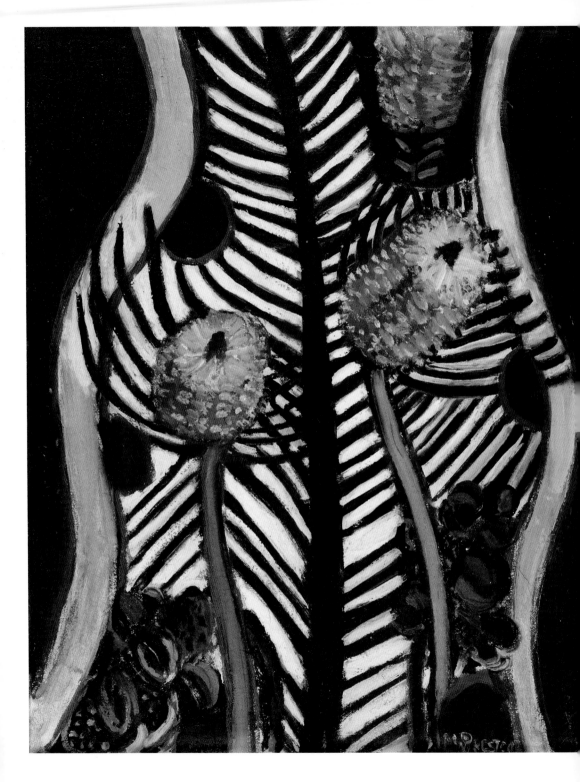

stencils on Aboriginal themes, native flora and Australian land-scapes, with many of them as abstracted as any images in her long career. Hundreds of people attended the opening, to which the artist arrived holding a wicker basket filled with flowers. The exhibition was a sell-out by the end of the first day, a comment not so much on the quality of the constituent prints themselves but on Preston's reputation. She observed on this occasion that her style had changed with the world around her,[20] though in many ways her art was ahead of its time. Not only did she embrace a multitude of disciplinary practices throughout her career, but she also considered and supported a place for 'other-ness' in Australian culture, advancing the causes of women's art and crafts, and celebrating Aboriginal art well before its wider appreciation began in the late 1960s and 1970s.

In writing about Preston's legacy shortly after her death in 1963, Hal Missingham commented, 'If Margaret Preston had been a man I feel sure she would have enjoyed a public reputation equally great as Dobell, Drysdale or Nolan in our time. But she was belligerently and seductively a woman; proud of it, imperi-ous in her demand that she be accepted'.[21] He would have been delighted to know that some fifty years later she is as much respected and loved as any of Australia's artists.

Banksia 1953

oil on canvas
48.8 × 65.3 cm
University of Newcastle
Collection
Presented to the Newcastle
Teachers College by teachers
attending post college
courses 1954

NOTES

INTRODUCTION

1 Hal Missingham, 'Margaret Preston', *Art and Australia* (Sydney), vol. 1, no. 2, August 1963, p. 90.
2 Terry Smith, *Modernism and Aboriginality, Transformations in Australian Art: The Twentieth Century—Modernism and Aboriginality*, Craftsman House, Sydney, 2002, p. 42.
3 John McDonald, *Federation: Australian Art and Society 1901–2001*, National Gallery of Australia, Canberra, 2001, p. 58.
4 Elizabeth Butel, *Margaret Preston: The Art of Constant Rearrangement*, Penguin, Melbourne, 1986, p. 7.
5 Margaret Preston, 'New Developments in Australian Art', *Australia National Journal* (Sydney), vol. 2, no. 6, 1 May 1941, p. 12.

1 BEGINNINGS

1 Margaret Preston, 'Why I Became a Convert to Modern Art', *The Home* (Sydney), vol. 4, no. 2, June 1923, p. 20. The question mark in parentheses is Preston's.
2 'Margaret Preston—Artist', *The Register News-Pictorial* (Adelaide), 14 September 1929, p. 3.
3 Norman Macgeorge, undated and unpublished manuscript, Norman Macgeorge papers, University of Melbourne Archives.
4 ibid.
5 ibid.
6 Margaret Preston, quoted in 'Margaret Preston's Two Artistic "Lives"', *The Sunday Herald* (Sydney), 3 September 1950, p. 11.
7 Margaret Preston, 'From Eggs to Electrolux', *Art in Australia*, Margaret Preston number, 3rd series, no. 22, December 1927, n.p. [p. 25].
8 Margaret Preston, quoted in 'Margaret Preston's Two Artistic "Lives"', p. 11.
9 Preston, 'From Eggs to Electrolux', n.p. [p. 25].
10 'Miss McPherson's Art Exhibition', *The Advertiser* (Adelaide), 11 September 1902, p. 10.
11 Preston, 'From Eggs to Electrolux', n.p. [p. 25].
12 'Two Girl Artists: An Interview by A. G. R.', *The Register* (Adelaide), 6 March 1907, p. 9.
13 'Exhibition of Paintings: Misses Macpherson and Davidson', *The Register* (Adelaide), 5 March 1907, p. 6.
14 ibid.
15 'Methodist Ladies College: Report of Head Mistress', *The Register* (Adelaide), 19 December 1908, p. 11.

16 Mrs Gordon, letter to Humphrey McQueen, 6 December 1977, cited in Ian North (ed.), *The Art of Margaret Preston*, Art Gallery Board of South Australia, Adelaide, p. 62.
17 Preston, 'From Eggs to Electrolux', n.p. [p. 27].
18 Margaret Macpherson, letter to Norman Carter, Île de Noirmoutier, 18 August 1913, Norman Carter papers, State Library of New South Wales, Sydney, MLMSS 471.
19 Margaret Preston, Aphorism no. 56, '92 Aphorisms by Margaret Preston and others', in Sydney Ure Smith and Leon Gellert (eds), *Margaret Preston: Recent Paintings*, Art in Australia, Sydney, 1929, n.p.
20 Macpherson, letter to Norman Carter, 18 August 1913.
21 Preston, 'From Eggs to Electrolux', n.p. [p. 26].
22 ibid., n.p. [p. 27].
23 Macpherson, letter to Norman Carter, 18 August 1913.

2 CRAFTS THAT AID

1 Clive Bell, *Art*, Chatto and Windus, London, 1914, p. 58.
2 'London Gossip', *The Register* (Adelaide), 9 April 1912, p. 5. There was contemporaneous coverage of Fry's exhibitions in the Victorian Artists Society journal and the New South Wales Institute of Architects circular, *The Salon*, for example.
3 The Steins persuaded their friend Harriet Levy to lend Matisse's *La femme aux yeux verts* (1908), a highlight of the exhibition, now in the collection of the Museum of Modern Art, San Francisco. Anna Gruetzner Robins, 'Manet and the Post-Impressionists: A Checklist of Exhibits', *The Burlington Magazine*, December 2010, p. 793.
4 Roger Fry, 'The French Post-Impressionists', first published as the preface to the catalogue of the *Second Post-Impressionist Exhibition*, Grafton Galleries, London, 1912. JB Bullen (ed.), *Roger Fry: Vision and Design*, Oxford University Press, London, 1981, p. 167.
5 Preston, 'Eggs to Electrolux', n.p. [p. 28].
6 Ross McMullin, *Farewell, Dear People*, Scribe Publications, Melbourne, 2012, p. 484.
7 Roger Butler, *The Prints of Margaret Preston: A Catalogue Raisonné*, National Gallery of Australia, Canberra, 2005, p. 12.

8 ibid.
9 Gladys Osborne, 'Reynella Pottery', in Louise Brown, Beatrix de Crespigny, Mary Harris, Kathleen Kyfflin Thomas and Phebe Watson (eds), *A Book of South Australia: Women in the First Hundred Years*, Rigby for the Women's Centenary Council of South Australia, Adelaide, 1936, p. 214.
10 Noris Ioannou, *Ceramics in South Australia 1836–1986: From Folk to Studio Pottery*, Wakefield Press, Adelaide, 1986, illustrated p. 360.
11 Margaret Preston, 'Crafts that Aid', *Art in Australia* (Sydney), 3rd series, no. 77, p. 26.
12 ibid., p. 27.
13 ibid., p. 28.
14 ibid., p. 29.

3 MARGARET'S KITCHEN

1 Leon Gellert, 'Margaret Preston was One of the Greats', *Sunday Telegraph* (Sydney), 8 January 1967, p. 14.
2 Daniel Thomas, 'Margaret Preston: Some Biographical Details Obtained from Her Widower WG Preston', 21 August 1963, Art Gallery of New South Wales Archive, Sydney.
3 'Art Exhibition Opened by the Governor', *The Advertiser* (Adelaide), 16 September 1919, p. 10.
4 '"Australia for artists": MacPherson–Reynell exhibition', *The Journal* (Adelaide), 15 September 1919, p. 1.
5 Grace Cochrane, *The Crafts Movement in Australia: A History*, New South Wales University Press, Sydney, 1992, p. 42.
6 Margaret Preston, quoted in 'Margaret Preston's Two Artistic "Lives"', p. 11.
7 Leon Gellert, 'Every Picture Tells a Story', *The Sydney Morning Herald*, 30 July 1939, p. 8.
8 'Margaret Preston, Artist', *The Mail* (Adelaide), 18 August 1923, p. 23.
9 ibid.
10 'Dozing Off Under the Best Conditions', *The Home* (Sydney), 1 July 1926, p. 21.
11 'We Assemble Here to Emphatically Denounce', *The Home* (Sydney), 1 June 1928, p. 27.
12 Margaret Preston, 'Away with Poker-Worked Kookaburras and Gumleaves!', *Daily Telegraph Sunday Pictorial* (Sydney), 6 April 1930, p. 22.
13 Margaret Preston, 'The Application of Aboriginal Designs', *Art in Australia* (Sydney), 3rd series, no. 31, March 1930, p. 44. Preston points to the author in the text.
14 The recipe book is held in the National Gallery of Australia collection. While the gallery has ascribed a date of c. 1915, traceable recipes clipped from

newspapers date from the early 1920s through to the early 1930s, suggesting the book was in long-term use. Further clipped recipes are contained in a scrapbook in the same collection.
15 Margaret Preston, 'Away with Poker-Worked Kookaburras and Gumleaves!', p. 22
16 'Art Exhibitions: Contemporary Painters', *The Sydney Morning Herald*, 29 November 1928, p. 15.
17 Treania Smith, quoted in Daniel Thomas, *The Treania Smith Collection*, exhibition catalogue, The Painters Gallery, Sydney, 1985, p. 11.
18 'Margaret Preston's Two Artistic "Lives"', p. 11.

4 ART BEGINS AT *HOME*

1 Thea Proctor, 'An Artist's Appreciation of Margaret Preston', *Art in Australia* (Sydney), Margaret Preston number, 3rd series, no. 22, December 1927, n.p. [p. 12].
2 Vernon Adams, 'She has Wanderlust', *A.M.* (Sydney), December 1948, p. 33.
3 Michael Bogle, *Design in Australia 1880–1970*, Craftsman House, Sydney, 1998, p. 58.
4 Sydney Ure Smith, editorial, *The Home* (Sydney), Interior Decoration number, 1 August 1929, p. 26.
5 Sydney Ure Smith, editorial, *Art in Australia* (Sydney), Margaret Preston number, 3rd series, no. 22, December 1927, n.p. [p. 3].
6 Margaret Preston to Mr Connor, Mosman, 8 January 1928, copy in Margaret Preston papers, Art Gallery of New South Wales Archive, Sydney.
7 Nancy Underhill, *Making Australian Art 1916–49: Sydney Ure Smith, Patron and Publisher*, Oxford University Press, Melbourne, 1991, p. 161.
8 ibid.
9 'Pet Pleasures and Private Prejudices', *The Home* (Sydney), 2 January 1928, p. 20.
10 Underhill, pp. 164–7.
11 R Haughton James, 'The Designer in Industry: A Serious National Need', *Australia National Journal* (Sydney), no. 1, winter, 1939, pp. 87, 91.

5 RECIPES FOR ART

1 Humphrey McQueen, *The Black Swan of Trespass: The Emergence of Modernist Painting in Australia to 1944*, Alternative Publishing Cooperative, Sydney, 1979, p. 152.
2 Margaret Preston, 'Pottery as a Profession', *Art in Australia* (Sydney), 3rd series, no. 32, June–July 1930, n.p.
3 'Utensils and Pottery', *The ABC Weekly* (Sydney), 28 June 1941, p. 47.
4 Margaret Preston, 'Pottery as a Profession', n.p.
5 Margaret Preston, letter to Mrs Heysen, Mosman,

20 October 1931, Hans Heysen papers, National Library of Australia, Canberra, MS 5071/1/2354.

6 Margaret Preston, 'Basket Weaving for the Amateur', *The Home* (Sydney), vol. 13, no. 8, August 1932, p. 46.

7 Margaret Preston, 'Wood-Blocking as a Craft', *Art in Australia*, 3rd series, no. 34, October–November 1934, p. 27.

8 Joyce Burns Glen, 'Outback Yields Art: Preston Painting Famous', *Christian Science Monitor* (Boston), 20 January 1954, p. 10.

9 Margaret Preston, 'Coloured Woodprints', *Woman's World* (Melbourne), vol. 6, no. 2, January 1926, p. 64.

10 ibid.

11 Deborah Edwards and Rose Peel with Denise Mimmocchi, *Margaret Preston*, exhibition catalogue, Art Gallery of New South Wales, Sydney, 2005, p. 82.

12 Proctor, n.p. [p. 16].

13 Margaret Preston, quoted in 'Distinguished Artist to Show 1953 Work', *The Sunday Herald* (Sydney), 20 September 1953, p. 27.

14 Butler, p. 67.

15 Margaret Preston, 'Some Silk Screen Methods', *Society of Artists Book*, Ure Smith, Sydney, 1947, pp. 22–3, 26–7, 30–1.

16 Claudio Alcorso, 'Foreword', *A New Approach to Textile Designing by a Group of Australian Artists*, Ure Smith Pty Ltd, Sydney, 1947, p. 3.

17 'Well Known Artists Style Fabrics', *The Australian Women's Weekly* (Sydney), 30 August 1947, p. 44.

18 Margaret Preston, quoted in Alcorso, *A New Approach to Textile Designing by a Group of Australian Artists*, p. 14.

19 Claudio Alcorso, quoted in transcript of panel session, 'Claudio Alcorso: The Experiment that Failed', *Artlink* (Adelaide), vol. 9, no. 4, summer, 1989–90, p. 15.

20 Sydney Ure Smith, 'Vision and Confidence in Art for Textiles', in Alcorso, *A New Approach to Textile Designing by a Group of Australian Artists*, p. 8.

21 Hal Missingham, 'Margaret Preston', *Art and Australia* (Sydney), vol. 1, no. 2, August 1963, p. 96.

22 Margaret Preston, 'Artists' Groundwork', *Society of Artists Book*, Ure Smith, Sydney, 1944, pp. 38–40.

6 THE GENTLE ART OF ARRANGING FLOWERS

1 Maurice Denis, 'Cézanne', trans. Roger Fry, *The Burlington Magazine* (London), vol. 16, no. 82, January 1910, p. 219.

2 Margaret Preston, 'An Exhibition 1933', *Manuscripts* (Geelong), no. 4, February 1933, p. 45.

3 Margaret Preston, Aphorism no. 46 in '92 Aphorisms by Margaret Preston and Others', in Sydney Ure Smith and Leon Gellert (eds), *Margaret Preston: Recent Paintings*, Art in Australia, Sydney, 1929, n.p.

4 'The Artist Who Changed Her Name', *Woman's Budget* (Sydney), 16 December 1931, p. 5.

5 *The Australasian* (Melbourne), 14 August 1920, p. 341, cited in Butler, p. 15.

6 A Radcliffe-Brown, 'Margaret Preston and Transition', *Art in Australia* (Sydney), Margaret Preston number, 3rd series, no. 22, December 1927, n.p. [p. 11]

7 Proctor, n.p. [p. 16].

8 ibid.

9 Thea Proctor and Margaret Preston, 'The Gentle Art of Flower Arranging', *The Home* (Sydney), vol. 5, no. 2, 1 June 1924, pp. 38–41.

10 'Intimate Jottings by Caroline', *The Australian Women's Weekly* (Sydney), 10 April 1937, p. 31.

11 Elizabeth Butel gave her first book on Preston this title: *Margaret Preston: The Art of Constant Rearrangement*; see also Edwards and Peel with Mimmocchi, p. 66.

12 Preston, 'Why I Became a Convert to Modern Art', p. 20.

13 Margaret Preston, 'Colour', *Art in Australia*, 3rd series, no. 9, October 1924, p. 23.

14 See Lesley Harding and Sue Cramer, *Cubism and Australian Art*, The Miegunyah Press, Melbourne, 2009, pp. 29–35.

15 Curator and art historian Ann Stephen made this discovery, see 'Introduction' in *Modern Times: The Untold Story of Modernism in Australia*, The Miegunyah Press, Melbourne, 2008, p. xxv.

16 Terry Smith first pointed out this connection in the essay 'Adopt, Adapt, Transform! Modernist Strategies in Margaret Preston's *Still life*, 1927', in his *Transformations in Australian Art: The Twentieth Century—Modernism and Aboriginality*, pp. 47–73. Smith points out that the distribution map for *L'Esprit Nouveau* on the back of no. 17 showed subscribers in Australia in 1923–24.

17 Edwards and Peel with Mimmocchi, p. 61.

18 'Life's Movie Show. Being Glimpses Here and There', *The Observer* (Adelaide), 10 March 1928, p. 61.

19 Preston, 'From Eggs to Electrolux', n.p. [p. 28].

20 '"I am not a flower": Mrs Preston's Art Gallery Portrait', *The Sun* (Sydney), 6 April 1930, p. 42.

21 Hal Missingham, 'Margaret Preston', p. 96.

7 BEAUTIFUL BEROWRA

1 Margaret Preston, letter to Basil Burdett, Scottish Hospital, Paddington, Sydney, 27 July 1928: 'Dr MacCormack says I'll be fit for anything soon—we'll see'. Margaret Preston papers, Art Gallery of New South Wales Archive, Sydney.

2 Census Bulletin no. 35: 'Population and Occupied Dwellings in Localities', Census of the Commonwealth of Australia, 30 June 1933, Australian Government, Canberra, 1933, p. 10.

3 Rhonda Davis, *Berowra Visions: Margaret Preston and Beyond*, exhibition catalogue, Macquarie University Art Gallery, Sydney, 2005, p. 30.

4 Margaret Preston, 'Meccano as an Ideal', *Manuscripts* (Geelong), no. 2, November 1932, p. 90.

5 Davis, p. 30.

6 'An Air of Space ...', *The Sydney Morning Herald*, 10 November 1933, p. 4.

7 The Prestons purchased part of lot 59 and lot 60 Stewarts Road, Berowra, from Eliza Stewart. The land was consolidated into one title on 11 April 1932. Certificate of title volume 2151, folio 165 and volume 4526, folio 84, New South Wales Land and Property Information, Sydney.

8 Nora Cooper, 'Margaret Preston at Home', *The Australian Home Beautiful* (Melbourne), 1 February 1937, p. 32.

9 'An Air of Space ...', p. 4.

10 Cooper, p. 52.

11 'An Air of Space ...', p. 4.

12 Bulletin Board, *The Australian Home Beautiful* (Melbourne), 1 February 1937, p. 5.

13 'Women Artists Who are Outstanding Exhibitors at this Year's Society of Artists Show', *The Sydney Morning Herald*, 13 September 1933, p. 5.

14 Mick Joffe, *Yarns and Photos: Beautiful Old Berowra and Hornsby to the Hawkesbury*, Sandstone Press, Berowra Heights, New South Wales, 1992, p. 126.

15 Edwards and Peel with Mimmocchi, p. 151.

16 Mrs PR Ladd, interview by Ian North, 18 February 1980, cited in Ian North (ed.), *The Art of Margaret Preston*, p. 14.

17 Davis, p. 32.

18 ibid., p. 43.

19 John Huxley, 'The Pot that Nearly Spoilt a Moment in Art', *The Sydney Morning Herald*, 21 September 2002.

20 Myra Payne (née Worrell), letter to Mick Joffe, 26 December 1973, private collection.

21 ibid.

22 Margaret Preston, letter to John Young, Berowra, n.d. [1934], Margaret Preston papers, Art Gallery of New South Wales Archive, Sydney.

23 Eric Riddell, notes from telephone interview with 'Chum', resident of Berowra, September 2004, Margaret Preston papers, Art Gallery of New South Wales Archive, Sydney.

24 Margaret Preston, quoted in Cooper, pp. 31–2.

8 SEARCHING FOR THE MAGIC LANTERN

1 Edwards and Peel with Mimmocchi, p. 188.

2 Margaret Preston, 'What Is to Be Our National Art?', *Undergrowth: A Magazine of Youth and Ideals* (Sydney), March–April 1927, n.p.

3 Margaret Preston, 'Art for Crafts: Aboriginal Art Artfully Applied', *The Home* (Sydney), vol. 5, no. 5, 1 December 1924, pp. 30–1; and Margaret Preston, 'The Indigenous Art of Australia', *Art in Australia* (Sydney), 3rd series, no. 11, March 1925, pp. 32–45.

4 Preston, 'Away with Poker-Worked Kookaburras and Gumleaves!', p. 22.

5 Margaret Preston, 'An Art in the Beginning', *Society of Artists Book*, Ure Smith, Sydney, 1945–46, p. 19.

6 Preston, 'Away with Poker-Worked Kookaburras and Gumleaves!', p. 22

7 Preston, 'The Indigenous Art of Australia', p. 34.

8 Pablo Picasso, quoted in Anne Ganteführer-Trier, *Cubism*, Taschen, Cologne, 2006, p. 45.

9 Margaret Preston, quoted in Vernon Adams, 'She has Wanderlust', *A.M.* (Sydney), December 1948, p. 33.

10 Edwards and Peel with Mimmocchi, p. 164.

11 Margaret Preston, 'Aboriginal Art', *Art in Australia* (Sydney), 4th series, no. 2, 1 June 1941, p. 46.

12 Preston, 'An Art in the Beginning', p. 19.

13 'The Artist after the War', *Studio of Realist Art* (Sydney), no. 2, 10 May 1945, p. 1.

14 Kenneth Gifford, *Jindyworobak: Towards an Australian Culture*, Jindyworobak, Melbourne, 1944, p. 18.

15 Butel, p. 62.

16 Margaret Preston, letter to Lionel Lindsay, Margaret Preston papers, Art Gallery of New South Wales Archive, Sydney.

17 Butel, p. 62.

18 Adams, p. 33.

19 'Distinguished Artist to Show 1953 Work', *The Sunday Herald* (Sydney), 20 September 1953, p. 27.

20 ibid.

21 Hal Missingham, 'Margaret Preston', p. 100.

SELECT BIBLIOGRAPHY

BOOKS

Alcorso, Claudio, *A New Approach to Textile Designing by a Group of Australian Artists*, Ure Smith, Sydney, 1947.

Ambrus, Caroline, *Australian Women Artists. First Fleet to 1945: History, Hearsay and Her Say*, Irrepressible Press, Canberra, 1992.

Bannerman, Colin, *A Friend in the Kitchen: Old Australian Cookery Books*, Kangaroo Press, Sydney, 1996.

Bell, Clive, *Art*, Chatto and Windus, London, 1914.

Bogle, Michael, *Design in Australia 1880–1970*, Craftsman House, Sydney, 1998.

Bogle, Michael, *Designing Australia: Readings in the History of Design*, Pluto Press, Sydney, 2002.

Brown, Louise, Beatrix de Crespigny, Mary Harris, Kathleen Kyfflin Thomas and Phebe Watson (eds), *A Book of South Australia: Women in the First Hundred Years*, Rigby for the Women's Centenary Council of South Australia, Adelaide, 1936.

Butel, Elizabeth, *Margaret Preston: The Art of Constant Rearrangement*, Penguin, Melbourne, 1986.

Butler, Rex (ed.), *Radical Revisionism: An Anthology of Writings on Australian Art*, IMA Publishing, Brisbane, 2005.

Butler, Roger, *The Prints of Margaret Preston: A Catalogue Raisonné*, National Gallery of Australia, Canberra, 2005.

Campbell, Jean, *Early Sydney Moderns: John Young and the Macquarie Galleries 1916–1946*, Craftsman House, Sydney, 1988.

Cochrane, Grace, *The Crafts Movement in Australia: A History*, New South Wales University Press, Sydney, 1992.

Dever, Maryanne (ed.), *Wallflowers and Witches: Women and Culture in Australia 1910–1945*, University of Queensland Press, Brisbane, 1994.

Eagle, Mary, *Australian Modern Painting between the Wars 1914–1939*, Bay Books, Sydney, 1989.

Ganteführer-Trier, Anne, *Cubism*, Taschen, Cologne, Germany, 2006.

Gifford, Kenneth, *Jindyworobak: Towards an Australian Culture*, Jindyworobak, Melbourne, 1944.

Grishin, Sasha, *Australian Art: A History*, Miegunyah Press, Melbourne, 2015.

Harding, Lesley, and Sue Cramer, *Cubism and Australian Art*, Miegunyah Press, Melbourne, 2009.

Harrison, Charles, *English Art and Modernism 1900–1993*, Allen Lane and Indiana University Press, London and Bloomington, IN, 1981.

Hassell, Geoff, *Camberwell School of Arts and Crafts: Its Students and Teachers 1943–1960*, Antique Collectors' Club, Woodbridge, UK, 1988.

Hill, Valerie, *The Cazneaux Women*, Craftsman House, Sydney, 2000.

Hoorn, Jeanette (ed.), *Strange Women: Essays in Art and Gender*, Melbourne University Press, Melbourne, 1994.

Hoyle, John, *An Annotated Bibliography of Australian Domestic Cookery Books, 1860s to 1950s*, Billycan Cook, Sydney, 2010.

Ioannou, Noris, *Ceramics in South Australia 1836–1986: From Folk to Studio Pottery*, Wakefield Press, Adelaide, 1986.

Joffe, Mick, *Yarns and Photos: Beautiful Old Berowra and Hornsby to the Hawkesbury*, Sandstone Press, Berowra Heights, NSW, 1992.

Johnson, Heather, *The Sydney Art Patronage System 1890–1940*, Bungoona Technologies, Sydney, 1997.

Kerr, Joan (ed.), *Heritage: The National Women's Art Book, 500 works by 500 Australian Women Artists from Colonial Times to 1955*, Art and Australia, Sydney, 1995.

Little, Penelope, *A Studio in Montparnasse. Bessie Davidson: An Australian Artist in Paris*, Craftsman House, Melbourne, 2003.

McCaughey, Patrick, *Strange Country: Why Australian Painting Matters*, Miegunyah Press, Melbourne, 2014.

McLean, Ian, *White Aborigines: Identity Politics in Australian Art*, Cambridge University Press, Cambridge, UK, and New York, NY, 1998.

McMullin, Ross, *Farewell, Dear People: Biographies of Australia's Lost Generation*, Scribe Publications, Melbourne, 2012.

McQueen, Humphrey, *The Black Swan of Trespass: The Emergence of Modernist Painting in Australia to 1944*, Alternative Publishing Cooperative, Sydney, 1979.

Monro, Amie, *The Practical Australian Cookery: A Collection of Up-to-Date Tried Recipes for Domestic and General Use*, Dymocks Book Arcade, Sydney, 1914.

North, Ian (ed.), *The Art of Margaret Preston*, Art Gallery Board of South Australia, Adelaide, 1980.

Smith, Terry, *Transformations in Australian Art: The Twentieth Century—Modernism and Aboriginality*, Craftsman House, Sydney, 2002.

Stephen, Ann, Philip Goad and Andrew McNamara (eds), *Modernism and Australia: Documents on Art, Design and Architecture 1917–1967*, Miegunyah Press, Melbourne, 2006.

Stephen, Ann, Philip Goad and Andrew McNamara (eds), *Modern Times: The Untold Story of Modernism in Australia*, Miegunyah Press, Melbourne, 2008.

Topliss, Helen, *Modernism and Feminism: Australian Women Artists 1900–1940*, Craftsman House, Sydney, 1996.

Underhill, Nancy, *Making Australian Art 1916–49: Sydney Ure Smith, Patron and Publisher*, Oxford University Press, Melbourne, 1991.

Ure Smith, Sydney (ed.), *Australian Present Day Art*, Ure Smith, Sydney, 1943.

Ure Smith, Sydney (ed.), *Margaret Preston's Monotypes*, Ure Smith, Sydney, 1949.

Ure Smith, Sydney, and Leon Gellert (eds), *Margaret Preston: Recent Paintings*, Art in Australia, Sydney, 1929.

Walker, Henrietta, *Profitable Hobbies: Hooked Rugs, Bark, Flax and Rafia Work*, Lloyd Jones Printing, Melbourne, n.d. [c. 1920].

Walker, Henrietta, *Rafia Work: A Simple Craft with Great Possibilities*, Whitcombe and Tombs, Melbourne, n.d. [1913].

Wilson, Shirley Cameron, *From Shadow into Light: South Australian Women Artists Since Colonisation*, Pagel Books, Adelaide, 1988.

EXHIBITION CATALOGUES

Cashman, Katrina, *Margaret Preston in Mosman*, Mosman Art Gallery, Sydney, 2002.

Davis, Rhonda, *Berowra Visions: Margaret Preston and Beyond*, Macquarie University Art Gallery, Sydney, 2005.

Edwards, Deborah, and Denise Mimmocchi (eds), *Sydney Moderns: Art for a New World*, Art Gallery of New South Wales, Sydney, 2013.

Edwards, Deborah, and Rose Peel with Denise Mimmocchi, *Margaret Preston*, Art Gallery of New South Wales, Sydney, 2005.

Fry, Roger, 'The French Post-Impressionists', first published as the preface to the catalogue of the *Second Post-Impressionist Exhibition*, Grafton Galleries, London, 1912; reproduced in JB Bullen (ed.), *Roger Fry: Vision and Design*, Oxford University Press, London, 1981.

Gott, Ted, Laurie Benson and Sophie Matthiesson, *Modern Britain 1900–1960: Masterworks from Australian and New Zealand Collections*, National Gallery of Victoria, Melbourne, 2007.

Hylton, Jane, *South Australian Women Artists: Painting from the 1890s to the 1940s*, Art Gallery Board of South Australia, Adelaide, 1994.

McDonald, John, *Federation: Australian Art and Society 1901–2001*, National Gallery of Australia, Canberra, 2001.

North, Ian (ed.), *The Art of Margaret Preston*, Art Gallery Board of South Australia, Adelaide, 1980.

Thea Proctor and Margaret Preston, Grosvenor Galleries, Sydney, 1925.

Thomas, Daniel, *The Treania Smith Collection*, The Painters Gallery, Sydney, 1985.

PERIODICAL AND NEWSPAPER ARTICLES

Adams, Vernon, 'She Has Wanderlust', *A.M.* (Sydney), December 1948, p. 33.

'An Air of Space ...', *The Sydney Morning Herald*, 10 November 1933, p. 4.

'Art Accent in Textile Show', *The Sydney Morning Herald*, 21 August 1947, p. 13.

'Art Exhibition Opened by the Governor', *The Advertiser* (Adelaide), 16 September 1919, p. 10.

'Art Exhibitions: Contemporary Painters', *The Sydney Morning Herald*, 29 November 1928, p. 15.

'The Art of Margaret Preston', *The Age* (Melbourne), 18 January 1930, p. 4.

'The Artist after the War', *Studio of Realist Art* (Sydney), no. 2, 10 May 1945, p. 1.

'The Artist Who Changed Her Name', *Woman's Budget* (Sydney), 16 December 1931, p. 5.

'"Australia for Artists": MacPherson–Reynell Exhibition', *The Journal* (Adelaide), 15 September 1919, p. 1.

Britton, Stephanie (ed.), 'Panel Session: Claudio Alcorso: The Experiment that Failed', *Artlink* (Adelaide), vol. 9, no. 4, summer, 1989–90, pp. 13–15.

Bulletin Board, *The Australian Home Beautiful* (Melbourne), 1 February 1937, p. 5.

Butler, Roger, 'A Garden of Rest. Margaret Preston's Berowra Garden', *Australian Garden History* (Melbourne), vol. 10, no. 2, 1998, pp. 9–14.

Butler, Roger, 'Margaret Preston—Response to Berowra', *Imprint* (Melbourne), vol. 22, nos 1–2, 1987, pp. 18–19.

Census Bulletin no. 35: 'Population and Occupied Dwellings in Localities', Census of the Commonwealth of Australia, 30 June 1933, Australian Government, Canberra, 1933.

Cooper, Nora, 'Margaret Preston at Home', *The Australian Home Beautiful* (Melbourne), 1 February 1937, pp. 28–32, 52.

Davis, Rhonda, 'Margaret Preston's Rugs', *Art and Australia* (Sydney), vol. 43, no. 1, spring, 2005, pp. 108–9.

Denis, Maurice, 'Cézanne', Roger Fry (trans.), *The Burlington Magazine* (London), vol. 16, no. 82, January 1910, pp. 207–19.

'A Difficult Medium: Margaret Preston's Monotypes', *The Age* (Melbourne), 6 August 1949, p. 8.

'Distinguished Artist to Show 1953 Work', *The Sunday Herald* (Sydney), 20 September 1953, p. 27.

'Dozing off Under the Best Conditions', *The Home* (Sydney), vol. 7, no. 7, 1 July 1926, pp. 20–21.

Eagle, Mary, 'Australian Painters in France: 1890s to 1920s', in Anne-Marie Nisbet and Maurice Blackman (eds), *The French-Australian Cultural Connection*, University of New South Wales, Sydney, 1984.

Eagle, Mary, 'Multiple Contexts in the First Decades of the Twentieth Century', *Journal of Art Historiography* (Birmingham, UK), vol. 4, 2001.

'Exhibition of Paintings: Misses Macpherson and Davidson', *The Register* (Adelaide), 5 March 1907, p. 6.

Finlayson, Ronald, 'Margaret R. McPherson', *Art in Australia* (Sydney), 3rd number, November 1917, n.p.

Gellert, Leon, 'Every Picture Tells a Story', *The Sydney Morning Herald*, 30 July 1939, p. 8.

Gellert, Leon, 'Margaret Preston Was One of the Greats', *Sunday Telegraph* (Sydney), 9 January 1967, p. 14.

Glen, Joyce Burns, 'Outback Yields Art: Preston Painting Famous', *Christian Science Monitor* (Boston), 20 January 1954, p. 10.

Goodchild, John C, 'Pottery', *Manuscripts* (Geelong), no. 3, November 1932, pp. 25–8.

Gruetzner Robins, Anna, 'Manet and the Post-Impressionists: A Checklist of Exhibits', *The Burlington Magazine* (London), no. 1293, December 2010, pp. 782–93.

Haughton James, R, 'The Designer in Industry: A Serious National Need', *Australia National Journal* (Sydney), no. 1, winter, 1939, pp. 87, 91.

Huxley, John, 'The Pot that Nearly Spoilt a Moment in Art', *The Sydney Morning Herald*, 21 September 2002.

'"I am not a flower": Mrs Preston's Art Gallery Portrait', *The Sun* (Sydney), 6 April 1930, p. 42.

'Intimate Jottings by Caroline', *The Australian Women's Weekly* (Sydney), 10 April 1937, p. 31.

Lejeune, Philippe, Annette Tomarken and Edward Tomarken, 'Autobiography in the Third Person', *New Literary History* (Charlottesville, VA), vol. 9, no. 1, autumn, 1977, pp. 27–50.

'Let's Talk of Interesting People', *The Australian Women's Weekly* (Sydney), 17 April 1937, p. 2.

'Life's Movie Show. Being Glimpses Here and There', *The Observer* (Adelaide), 10 March 1928, p. 61.

'London Gossip', *The Register* (Adelaide), 9 April 1912, p. 5.

McCarthy, Frederick, 'Aboriginal Art', *Art in Australia* (Sydney), 3rd series, no. 77, 15 November 1939, pp. 53–62.

McConnel, Ursula, 'Inspiration and Design in Aboriginal Art', *Art in Australia* (Sydney), 3rd series, no. 59, 15 May 1935, pp. 49–68.

McIntyre, Arthur, 'The Art of Margaret Preston', *Art and Australia*, vol. 18, no. 3, autumn, 1981, pp. 220–3.

McKenzie, Janet, 'Beyond Bloomsbury: Designs of the Omega Workshops, 1913–19', *Studio International*, www.studiointernational.com/index.php/beyond-bloomsbury-designs-of-the-omega-workshops-1913-ndash-19 (viewed 10 March 2016).

McLean, Ian, 'Aboriginalism: White Aborigines and Australian Nationalism', *Australian Humanities Review* (Melbourne), no. 10, May 1998, http://australianhumanitiesreview.org/1998/05/01/issue-10-may-1998/ (viewed 20 January 2016).

McNeil, Peter, 'Decorating the Home: Australian Interior Decoration between the Wars', *Art and Australia* (Sydney), vol. 33, no. 2, summer, 1995, pp. 222–31.

McPhee, John, 'The Pottery of Margaret Preston and Gladys Reynell', *Craft Australia* (Sydney), summer, 1984, pp. 55–9.

Maloney, Shane, 'Thea Proctor and Margaret Preston', *The Monthly* (Melbourne), November 2008, p. 74.

'Margaret Preston, Artist', *The Mail* (Adelaide), 18 August 1923, p. 23.

'Margaret Preston—Artist', *The Register News-Pictorial* (Adelaide), 14 September 1929, p. 3.

'Margaret Preston—Master of Still Life', *The Home* (Sydney), vol. 10, no. 8, 1 August 1929, p. 20.

'Margaret Preston's Two Artistic "Lives"', *The Sunday Herald* (Sydney), 3 September 1950, p. 11.

Marrie, Adrian, 'Killing Me Softly: Aboriginal Art and Western Critics', *Art Network* (Sydney), no. 14, summer, 1985, pp. 17–21.

Meacham, Steve, 'Travel Brought out the Best at Home', *The Sydney Morning Herald*, 15 December 2004.

Menz, Christopher, '1946: Modernage Fabrics', *Craft Australia* (Sydney), no. 4, summer, 1987, pp. 72–7.

'Methodist Ladies College: Report of Head Mistress', *The Register* (Adelaide), 19 December 1908, p. 11.

Mimmocchi, Denise, and Deborah Edwards, 'Margaret Preston', *Art and Australia* (Sydney), vol. 43, no. 1, spring, 2005, pp. 100–7.

'Miss McPherson's Art Exhibition', *The Advertiser* (Adelaide), 11 September 1902 p. 10.

Missingham, Hal, 'Margaret Preston', *Art and Australia* (Sydney), vol. 1, no. 2, August 1963, pp. 90–101.

Missingham, Hal, 'A Note on the Art of Margaret Preston', *Colour Magazine, Sunday Sun Supplement* (Sydney), 14 April 1946, p. 11.

Moore, Catriona, 'Craftwork: Margaret Preston, Emily Carr and the Welfare Frontier', *ACH: The Journal of the History of Culture in Australia*, no. 25, 2006, pp. 57–81.

Moore, Catriona, 'Margaret Preston at Home', in Rex Butler (ed.), *Radical Revisionism: An Anthology of Writings on Australian Art*, IMA Publishing, Brisbane, 2005, pp. 200–12.

Moses, Alexa, 'Shadow Cast over a Painter's Legacy', *The Sydney Morning Herald*, 25 July 2005.

Norman, Julie, 'Names behind the Christmas Cards', *Woman* (Sydney), 27 December 1948, pp. 18–19.

'No "Tourist Art" for Margaret Preston', *The Sydney Morning Herald Women's Section*, 22 July 1954, p. 1.

O'Connell, Michael, 'Some Observations on Fabric Design', *Manuscripts* (Geelong), no. 3, November 1932, pp. 57–60.

Peel, Rose, 'Margaret Preston', *Style 1900* (Lamberville, NJ), vol. 15, no. 3, summer–fall, 2002, pp. 50–8.

Peers, Juliette, 'The Canon and its Discontents: Women Artists as Drivers of Early Art Historical Activities and Alternative Art Historical Narratives in Australia', *Journal of Art Historiography* (Birmingham, UK), no. 4, June 2011.

'Pet Pleasures and Private Prejudices', *The Home* (Sydney), vol. 9, no. 1, 2 January 1928, p. 20.

Proctor, Thea, 'An Artist's Appreciation of Margaret Preston', *Art in Australia* (Sydney), Margaret Preston number, 3rd series, no. 22, December 1927, n.p.

Radcliffe-Brown, Alfred, 'Margaret Preston and Transition', *Art in Australia* (Sydney), Margaret Preston number, 3rd series, no. 22, December 1927, n.p.

Rees, Lloyd 'N.S.W. Art Gallery Exhibitions: Margaret Preston', in *Society of Artists Book 1942*, Ure Smith, Sydney, 1942, p. 74.

'Should There Be an Australian Tariff on Imported Works of Art?', *Art in Australia* (Sydney), 3rd series, no. 8, June 1924, pp. 47, 50.

Smith, Terry, 'The Provincialism Problem', *Artforum* (New York, NY), vol. 13, no. 1, September 1974, pp. 54–9.

Stephen, Ann, 'Margaret Preston', in Joan Kerr (ed.), *Heritage: The National Women's Art Book, 500 Works by 500 Australian Women Artists from Colonial Times to 1955*, Art and Australia, Sydney, 1995.

Stephen, Ann, 'Margaret Preston's Second Coming', *Art Network* (Sydney), no. 2, spring, 1980, pp. 14–15.

'This Week's Prizewinners', *The Australian Women's Weekly* (Sydney), 15 January 1938, p. 6.

Thomas, Daniel, 'One Birth—and Two Deaths', *Sunday Telegraph* (Sydney), 2 June 1963, p. 43.

Tindale, Norman B, 'Primitive Art of the Australian Aborigines', *Manuscripts* (Geelong), no. 3, November 1932, pp. 38–42.

'Two Girl Artists: An Interview by A. G. R.', *The Register* (Adelaide), 6 March 1907, p. 9.

Ure Smith, Sydney, editorial, *Art in Australia* (Sydney), Margaret Preston number, 3rd series, no. 22, December 1927, n.p.

Ure Smith, Sydney, editorial, *The Home* (Sydney), Interior Decoration number, vol. 10, no. 8, 1 August 1929, p. 26.

'Utensils and Pottery', *ABC Weekly* (Sydney), 28 June 1941, p. 47.

Watson, Bronwyn, 'Public Works: Margaret Preston', *The Australian*, 9 July 2011.

'We Assemble Here to Emphatically Denounce', *The Home* (Sydney), vol. 9, no. 6, 1 June 1928, p. 27.

'Well Known Artists Style Fabrics', *The Australian Women's Weekly* (Sydney), 30 August 1947, p. 44.

'The Wide World of Mrs. Preston', *A.F.I.A. World* (US), summer, 1963, p. 5.

Williamson, Liz, 'Capturing the Landscape: Textiles for the Australian Fashion Industry', *Textile Society of America Symposium Proceedings*, University of Nebraska, Lincoln NE, paper 61, http://digitalcommons.unl.edu/tsaconf/61 (viewed 20 January 2016).

'Women Artists Who Are Outstanding Exhibitors at This Year's Society of Artists Show', *The Sydney Morning Herald*, 13 September 1933, p. 5.

ARTICLES BY MARGARET PRESTON

'Aboriginal Art', *Art in Australia* (Sydney), 4th series, no. 2, 1 June 1941, p. 46.

'American Art under the New Deal: Murals', *Art in Australia* (Sydney), 3rd series, no. 69, 15 November 1937, pp. 51–8.

'The Application of Aboriginal Designs', *Art in Australia* (Sydney), 3rd series, no. 31, March 1930, p. 44–57.

'Art for Crafts: Aboriginal Art Artfully Applied', *The Home* (Sydney), vol. 5, no. 5, 1 December 1924, pp. 30–1.

'An Art in the Beginning', *Society of Artists Book 1945–46*, Ure Smith, Sydney, 1946, pp. 14–19.

'Artists' Groundwork', *Society of Artists Book 1944*, Ure Smith, Sydney, 1944, pp. 38–40.

'Australian Artists Versus Art', *Art in Australia* (Sydney), 3rd series, no. 26, December 1928, n.p.

'Away with Poker-Worked Kookaburras and Gumleaves!', *Daily Telegraph Sunday Pictorial* (Sydney), 6 April 1930, p. 22.

'Basket Weaving for the Amateur', *The Home* (Sydney), vol. 13, no. 8, August 1932, pp. 46–7, 57, 59.

'Colour', *Art in Australia* (Sydney), 3rd series, no. 9, October 1924, pp. 18–23.

'Coloured Woodprints', *Woman's World* (Melbourne), vol. 6, no. 2, January 1926, pp. 64, 113.

'Crafts that Aid', *Art in Australia* (Sydney), 3rd series, no. 77, November 1939, pp. 26–30.

'An Exhibition 1933', *Manuscripts* (Geelong), no. 4, February 1933, pp. 45–9.

'Five Lectures Given in the National Art Gallery of N.S.W.', *Art in Australia* (Sydney), 3rd series, no. 72, 15 August 1938, pp. 48–52.

'Forming the Queue for Queensland', *The Home* (Sydney), 1 December 1927, pp. 36, 70, 72.

'From Eggs to Electrolux', *Art in Australia* (Sydney), Margaret Preston number, 3rd series, no. 22, December 1927, n.p.

'The Gentle Art of Flower Arranging', *The Home* (Sydney), vol. 5, no. 2, 1 June 1924, pp. 38–41 (co-authored with Thea Proctor).

'An Ideal Australian Tour', *The Home* (Sydney), 1 December 1926, p. 46.

'The Indigenous Art of Australia', *Art in Australia* (Sydney), 3rd series, no. 11, March 1925, pp. 32–43.

'Meccano as an Ideal', *Manuscripts* (Geelong), no. 2, November 1932, pp. 90–1.

'New Caledonia and New Hebrides', *The Home* (Sydney), 1 October 1928, pp. 32–5, 76.

'New Developments in Australian Art', *Australia National Journal* (Sydney), vol. 2, no. 6, 1 May 1941, pp. 12–13.

'Nothing but the East', *The Home* (Sydney), 2 January 1935, pp. 42–3, 78, 80.

'O! For Orange', *Australia National Journal* (Sydney), 1 March 1941, pp. 48–51.

'The Orientation of Art in the Post-War Pacific', *Society of Artists Book 1942*, Ure Smith, Sydney, 1942, pp. 7–9.

'Paintings in Arnhem Land', *Art in Australia* (Sydney), 3rd series, no. 81, 25 November 1940, pp. 58–63.

'Peiping and the Great Wall of China', *The Home*, 1 February 1935, pp. 26–7, 75.

'Pottery as a Profession', *Art in Australia* (Sydney), 3rd series, no. 32, June–July 1930, n.p.

'The Puppet Show of Osaka, Japan', *Manuscripts* (Melbourne), no. 12, 20 February 1935, pp. 15–17.

'Running around the Americas', *The Home* (Sydney), 1 November 1937, pp. 53–6, 74, 76, 79, 81.

'Some Silk Screen Methods', *Society of Artists Book 1946–47*, Ure Smith, Sydney, 1947, pp. 22–3, 26–7, 30–1.

'There and Back in Three Months', *The Home* (Sydney), 1 October 1926, pp. 31, 92.

'What Is to Be Our National Art?', *Undergrowth: A Magazine of Youth and Ideals* (Sydney), March–April 1927, n.p.

'Why I Became a Convert to Modern Art', *The Home* (Sydney), vol. 4, no. 2, June 1923, p. 20.

'Wood-Blocking as a Craft', *Art in Australia* (Sydney), 3rd series, no. 34, October–November 1930, pp. 27–35.

MANUSCRIPT MATERIAL AND UNPUBLISHED PAPERS

Hans Heysen papers, National Library of Australia, Canberra, MS 5073.

John Young papers and the Macquarie Galleries Archive, Art Gallery of New South Wales Archive, Sydney, MS 1995.99.

Macgeorge, Norman, unpublished manuscript, Norman Macgeorge papers, University of Melbourne Archives, Melbourne.

Margaret Preston papers, Art Gallery of New South Wales Archive, Sydney, MS 1963.1.

Margaret Preston papers, National Library of Australia, Canberra, MS 5116.

Norman St Clair Carter papers, State Library of New South Wales, Sydney, ML MSS 471.

Preston, Margaret, 'Australian Artist Speak', typescript of radio interview, c. 1947, National Gallery of Australia, Canberra.

Preston, William, interview with Hazel de Berg, c. 1962, Oral deB 6, Oral History Section, National Library of Australia, Canberra.

ACKNOWLEDGEMENTS

My foremost thanks go to the institutions and owners of works of art by Margaret Preston for their goodwill and kind permission to reproduce the images included here. I am most grateful to Nick Nicholson at the National Gallery of Australia, and Jenni Carter and Jude Fowler Smith at the Art Gallery of New South Wales, all of whom have offered much assistance with this book, and who work tirelessly and expertly behind the scenes to support the publishing of illustrated books and exhibition catalogues in Australia.

I would also like to thank Emma Busowsky Cox, Castlemaine Art Gallery and Historical Museum; Roger Butler and Rose Montebello, National Gallery of Australia; photographer Christian Capurro; Damian Cole, National Library of Australia; Helen Carroll, Wesfarmers Art Collection; Rebecca Coates, Shepparton Art Museum; Damian Cole, National Library of Australia; Tansy Curtin, Bendigo Art Gallery; Tessa Dorman, Menzies; Grant Eldridge, State Library of South Australia; Christine Feher, Royal Art Society of New South Wales; Sally Garrett, Cazneaux Estate; Brian Geraghty, Berowra Waters Inn; Melissa Hellard and Victoria Perin, Deutscher and Hackett; John Keats, Sotheby's Australia; Tracey Lock, Art Gallery of South Australia; Erica Persak and Sarah Yukich, Kerry Stokes Collection; John McPhee; Helen Manu, Ultimo College Library; Diane Morris, National Portrait Gallery; Mary Lou Byrne, Mosman Library Service; Jennie Rayner, Caroline Simpson Library & Research Collection, Sydney Living Museums; Gillean Shaw, University of Newcastle; Anastasia Symeonides, Fairfax Media; Richard Wotton, Sarjeant Gallery Te Whare o Rehua; and especially my colleague and friend Denise Mimmocchi, Art

Gallery of New South Wales. I am very grateful to Sue Cramer and Kendrah Morgan, who generously read early drafts of the text and offered much encouragement. My thanks also to Kirsty Grant, Linda Michael and Katarina Paseta at Heide Museum of Modern Art, and to Sigourney Jacks, who has graciously assisted in a multitude of ways.

Warm thanks to the wonderful Sally Heath and Cathy Smith, the executive publisher and the senior editor at MUP, also to Paige Amor, who brought much experience to editing the manuscript, and Hamish Freeman, who exercised both flair and restraint in designing a beautiful book.

A number of enthusiastic home cooks tested the recipes contained herein, and I thank them all for their efforts and suggestions: Molly Harding, Sally Heath, Sigourney Jacks, Judy McLeod, Sue Reynolds, Lynne Rahill, Jennifer Ross, Cathy Smith, Eliza Weichelt and Sarah Wilson. Special thanks to Jenny-Lynn Potter, who provided an early sounding board as well as preparing many Margaret Preston lunches, dinners, and afternoon teas.

I remain ever thankful to my parents, John and Molly Harding, who can be relied upon to offer sound and frank advice in tandem with unflinching support. And lastly my love and thanks to George, Olivia, Alex, and especially Eliza, who enjoyed this project as much as me.

IMAGE CREDITS

Images by Margaret Preston are © Margaret Rose Preston Estate, licensed by Viscopy Australia, 2016.

Margaret Preston's handwriting throughout is drawn from her recipe book held in the collection of the National Gallery of Australia. The colour tabs used on recipe pages are from her sketchbook on colour theory, also held in the National Gallery of Australia collection.

Images in private collections supplied as follows:

Pages 14, 16–17, 28, 30, 44, 76, 111, 113, 118, 145 courtesy Art Gallery of New South Wales; pages 12, 44 courtesy of Sotheby's Australia; page 63 courtesy of Menzies; pages 60 and 72 courtesy of Deutscher and Hackett; pages 102, 103, 122, 131, 160, 212 and 213 courtesy of Heide Museum of Modern Art; page 180 courtesy of Berowra Waters Inn.

Images from libraries supplied as follows:

Pages 101, 106 and 115 courtesy Caroline Simpson Library & Research Collection, Sydney Living Museums; pages 99 and 195 courtesy National Library of Australia, nla.obj-140219366 and nla.obj-140219817.

RECIPE INDEX

INDEX

THE MIEGUNYAH PRESS

THIS BOOK WAS DESIGNED AND TYPESET
BY PFISTERER + FREEMAN
THE TEXT WAS SET IN 10¼ POINT ARCHER
WITH 14½ POINTS OF LEADING
THE TEXT IS PRINTED ON 128 GSM MATT ART
THIS BOOK WAS EDITED BY PAIGE AMOR